The Marine Aquarists'

QUIZ BOOK

Martin and Barbara Moe

Green Turtle Publications
P.O Box 1800
Islamorada, FL 33036

Green Turtle Publications
P.O Box 1800
Islamorada, FL 33036

ISBN 0-939960-10-9

Printed in the United States of America

Contents

other books

by Martin A. Moe, Jr.

The Marine Aquarium Handbook :
Beginner to Breeder

The Marine Aquarium Reference :
Systems and Invertebrates

Lobsters :
Florida - Bahamas - the Caribbean

Breeding the Orchid Dottyback :
An Aquarist's Journal

Introduction

This is a book of multiple choice questions and answers. They pertain to marine aquariums, the life that we keep in aquariums, the natural marine environment, and the miscellanea that accompanies this hobby. It is set up in five sections of 80 questions each. The questions can be used to play various trivia or "20 questions" type games. It can also be used as a "test" of your knowledge, or as a pastime at club meetings, or even just as a source of information on the things of the hobby. We think that how ever you use this book, you will learn something about keeping marine life, the coral reefs, the great oceans, and marine aquaristics that you didn't know before.

The questions are not easy; okay, there are a few easy ones, but for the most part we wanted to make you think about the answer before jumping to a conclusion. They are all multiple choice and all have four choices. Always try to pick the best answer if more than one answer seems to be correct. We have tried very hard to make sure that only one answer is completely correct; for even if part of an answer is wrong, then, of course, that is not the correct answer. Often, you can use the process of elimination to find the correct answer, or at least narrow the choice down to two possibilities. A few of the questions are "true or false". And how can you have a true/false question with four choices for an answer? Well there are two "true" and two "false" answers, and if the statement is true, then you have to pick the correct true answer, and if false, then pick the correct false answer. You will have to think about these questions carefully before you give your final answer.

There are four questions on each right hand page. It is not necessary to fumble around at the back of the book for the answer, you just have to turn the page to check. You must not glance down the page to see the correct answer to questions you have not yet read. This is cheating and you may be severely reprimanded. If you do not handle temptation well, you may wish to use a paper to cover these answers.

When you take a test for a license or a grade in school, the questions should be fair and test your knowledge of a particular subject without strange and confusing twists and turns. Most of our questions are fair, but please note that you will receive neither grade nor license upon completion of the book. We have tried to include a brief explanation for each answer that provides a rationale and additional information. You may not agree with us all the time on the correct answer to a particular question (we didn't always agree ourselves), and if so, we are open to discussion.

We may do another book or two of this type if you enjoy this one. You might even have a suggestion for a question or topic that we might include. Drop us a line and let us know your thoughts. We won't be able to answer every communication, but we will appreciate them all.

Marine Fish

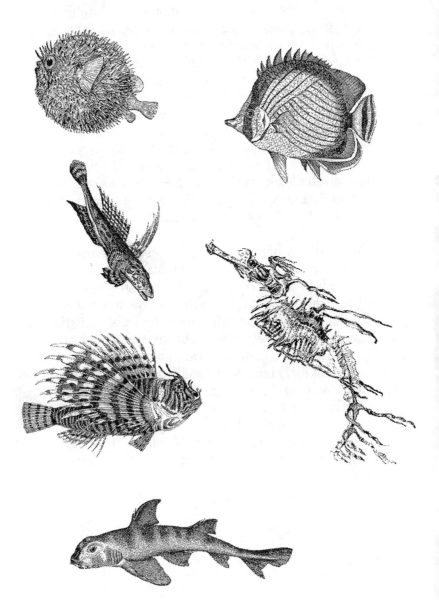

Marine Fish

Fish are amazing animals. They have an ancient lineage extending back to almost the dawn of the vertebrates, 500 million years in the past. They fill ecological niches from mountain top streams to the great ocean depths and vary in size from half inch gobies to the 60 foot, 20 ton whale shark. Some swim at speeds of almost 70 mph (sailfish), while others (frogfish) barely swim at all, spending their lives crawling along the sea floor. Dietary requirements are just as varied; some, like groupers, are quite catholic, feeding on almost anything that happens by; while others, like the bluestreak cleaner wrasse that feeds only on the external parasites of other fish, are so specific in their diet that they do not survive in captivity.

The relatively narrow ribbon of water that surrounds the land masses from the shore to water depths of 200 meters is home to 78% of all marine fish species (44% of all fishes), and it is in this area of the warm seas that we find those fish we call marine tropicals. Aquarists can now successfully keep in captivity a great many of these fish with astonishing variations of form, color, and behavior. Many books and articles on marine fish (with more on the way) are now available for aquarists, divers, and naturalists. So a well read marine fish aquarist should be able to correctly answer most of the questions in this section, right? Well, as my 8th grade science teacher Mr. Soper used to say, "Do your best, and good luck."

1. Male seahorses

  a) incubate the eggs and developing embryos in a brood pouch.

  b) are aggressive and may injure other males during the mating season.

  c) have unusual appendages known as saddlebags.

  d) like most other fish, use their tails to propel them through the water.

2. In the marine angelfish, family Pomacanthidae, there are about seven genera and 74 species. Of these, how many species are found in the tropical Atlantic?

  a) about half

  b) 25

  c) 9

  d) 52

3. In captivity, clownfish will spawn

  a) only in the presence of an anemone.

  b) only if the pair is in love.

  c) only if they are male and female.

  d) only if they are well fed.

4. Which is the best way to introduce a new fish to an aquarium where there may be conflict?

  a) Put him in and let them fight it out, they will soon learn to live with each other.

  b) Introduce the new fish at night so that he will already be familiar with the tank in the morning.

  c) Place him within a partition or box for a few days so that he will become familiar to the other fish.

  d) Keep the fish in the floating bag for a few days.

1. a) Male seahorses accept and fertilize the eggs from the female and place them in the brood pouch located on their abdomen. The young seahorses complete development in the brood pouch and are expelled by the male as fully formed juveniles. The posterior body and tail of seahorses forms a sort of prehensile tail which is used to hold the fish to the substrate rather than propel it through the water.

2. c) Most marine angelfish are found in the Pacific. There are relatively few species, only nine, that are found in the Atlantic. Even the Red Sea, a relatively small oceanic realm, has about 14 species of angelfish.

3. d) Clownfish will spawn under a variety of conditions, although a "sense of security" usually supplied by an anemone or a flower pot, and an absence of aggressive fish is most helpful in beginning the spawning cycle. Love is a human invention that only applies to fish as they are perceived within the human mind. Adequate nutrition, however, is essential for successful spawning. Rarely, two females may form a "pair" and spawn infertile eggs.

4. c) Depending on the size and species of the fish and the size of the tank, it is usually best to acclimate the new fish and the fish to each other before allowing them to directly interact. Adding a small fish to a large reef tank with lots of cover is an exception. Never, never leave a fish in the bag for more than a few minutes, just long enough to bring bag and tank temperatures to within a degree of each other. It is also a good idea not to add the bag water to the tank

5. Tank raised clownfish will not associate with an anemone unless they are introduced to the anemone within the first two months.

a) True, the mechanism that starts the development of the protective mucus is lost if not activated early.

b) False, clownfish are always protected from the stings of anemones.

c) True, the behavior pattern of symbiosis must be a part of early brain development.

d) False, the production of protective mucus following interaction with an anemone can occur at any time in the life cycle of the clownfish.

6. Fishes of the family Scaridae have the common name of parrotfish especially because

a) they are all brilliantly colored like parrots.

b) like parrots, they mimic the noises of other fish.

c) like parrots, they have large beak like mouths.

d) they can be trained to sit on one's shoulder.

7. To what fish does the term "pistol packin mamma" best apply?

a) the female clownfish

b) the watchman gobies

c) the great white shark

d) the green moray eel

8. The beautiful jewelfish, *Microspathodon chrysurus*, would be excellent aquarium fish if

a) they were not so aggressive.

b) they did not grow to such great size.

c) they were easy to feed.

d) they were more hardy.

5. d) While the exact nature and sequence of the behavioral and physiological processes that result in protection to the clownfish from the stinging cells of the anemone is not known, development of this protection is somewhat gradual and is not maintained if the clownfish does not constantly associate with an anemone.

6. c) Various species of parrot fish scrape the surface of rocks, crush corals, injest sediments and feed on various algae attached to these substrates. Their large, fused teeth form beak like mouths which are well suited for feeding on reef algae and corals. The pharyngeal mill, a second set of teeth, grinds up coral rock and reduces it to sandy sediments. Not all parrot fish are brilliantly colored, some are rather drab.

7. b) The watchman gobies (and the shrimp, prawn, and partner gobies) in the genera *Amblyeleotris, Cryptocentrus, Lotilia , Stonogobiops* and others have developed a mutualistic association with pistol (snapping) shrimp, *Alpheus* spp. The pistol shrimp builds a burrow and the goby lives and even spawns in the burrow built by the shrimp. In "return" the shrimp keeps an antenna on the goby when they are outside the burrow, and the goby warns the shrimp when a predator approaches. Both shrimp and goby then retreat back into the burrow.

8. a) The juvenile yellowtail damselfish, known as the jewelfish to aquarists because of the electric blue dots scattered over the dark body, is very aggressive to other fish and is thus difficult to keep in a small aquarium.

9. This is best way to quickly remove the parasitic dinoflagellate, *Amyloodinium ocellatum* from fish.

a) Give the fish a fresh water bath of 2 to 5 minutes, same temperature and pH as the tank water.

b) Use a copper treatment of 0.2 ppm in the tank for at least 3 weeks.

c) Gradually lower the salinity in the tank to 22 ppt (s.g. 1.0160) or slightly less and maintain this low salinity until all signs of the parasites are gone.

d) Use a very fine tipped forceps to individually remove each cyst. Be very careful around the gills.

10. A fish that is stenohaline

a) is never found in freshwater.

b) is never found in saltwater.

c) is always found in brackish water.

d) cannot abide great changes in salinity.

11. The Humahuma-nukanuka-a-puaa is

a) a triggerfish, *Rhinecantus sp.*

b) a Hawaiian wrasse, *Anamphses chrysocephalus.*

c) a Hawaiian term that beautifully describes the flowing motion of a school of triggerfish moving through a coral reef.

d) a channel between Hawaiian coral reefs.

12. Why is a spot near the tail of a fish (common in butterfly fish) called an "eye spot"?

a) It lines up with the eye of other fish and helps them to orient together in a school.

b) It looks like an eye and confuses predators.

c) It is an ocellus.

d) all of the above

9. a) Both b) and c) are effective treatments for this parasite, but a freshwater bath is the best way to immediately remove the parasites from an individual fish. Note: do not add the freshwater from the bath back to the aquarium with the fish. The best treatment for a fish only tank is to treat the tank with copper and perhaps the best treatment for a reef tank with copper sensitive invertebrates is to keep the tank fish free for over a month. This gives the cysts time to hatch and time for the resulting dinospores to die without finding a fish host.

10. d) The physiology of osmotic control (the internal regulation of salt content in body tissues) of most fish require that the fish remain in either a marine or freshwater environment, a condition known as stenohalinity.

11. a) These are the Hawaiian triggerfishes with the long name made famous in song. There are two species with the same common Hawaiian name, the lagoon triggerfish, *R. aculeatus*, and the reef triggerfish, *R. rectangulus*. Both species feed on algae and various invertebrates. The Hawaiian name means "triggerfish with a snout like a pig".

12. b) While it is true that "ocellus" is the term for a spot that looks like an eye, this is not why it is called an eye spot. The correct answer is that the "eye spot" or ocellus that appears on or near the tail of a fish is a marking that distracts predators by directing a predator's strike toward the tail rather than to the actual head of the potential prey.

14

13. Usually, with few exceptions, butterflyfish are not good inhabitants of reef tanks because

    a) they hide all the time.

    b) they often jump from the tank.

    c) most butterflyfish feed on corals.

    d) they are very aggressive to other fish.

14. Why do marine fish drink seawater?

    a) All animals have to drink water.

    b) Marine fish need freshwater and use "reverse osmosis" to remove the salt from saltwater.

    c) Fruit juice and sodas are not available underwater.

    d) They need a high salt content in their blood.

15. What gives the the puffer fish, family Tetraodontidae, their name?

    a) They feed on reef organisms and "puff" to remove sand and detritus from the reef before feeding.

    b) They can inhale large amounts of water when attacked by a predator, thus inflating their size several times and becoming impossible for the predator to swallow.

    c) They have addictive proclivities and smoke at least two packs a day.

    d) Their courtship includes a behavior where the male "puffs"at the female to stimulate her to release her eggs.

16. What is a gravid fish?

    a) a fish that is full with eggs

    b) a fish that lives on gravel beds

    c) a fish that is in the family Gravidae

    d) a fish that is seriously ill

13. c) Although there are a number of species of butterflyfish that are "reef safe", most butterflyfish feed on a number of species of hard and soft corals, and because of this, an aquarist should carefully research the feeding habits of any butterflyfish that are added to a reef tank. In many instances, butterflyfish do not eat in captivity, starve and then die. Young individuals are more adaptable to aquarium life than larger, older individuals.

14. b) Like all animals, marine fish require a constant supply of water for the functioning of all body processes. But the salt content of seawater is too high for vertebrate metabolism, so special cells in their gills excrete excess salt against an osmotic gradient (reverse osmosis) and their bodies maintain only the proper salt content, about one third the salinity of seawater. Note that some animals that live in very dry dessert conditions get water only from their food and do not drink liquid water.

15. b) As a form of defense to discourage predators, puffer fish, including the porcupinefish, *Diodon* spp., can greatly inflate their bodies with water; and in the case of the porcupinefish, this also erects spines located all over their bodies.

16. a) The term gravid refers to a female fish that has ovaries full with well developed eggs and is in a prespawning condition.

17. Obligate cleaner fish, like the cleaner wrasses, *Labroides* **spp.,**

 a) are a good addition to a marine aquarium.

 b) should only be in an aquarium with large fish.

 c) should be fed only live food.

 d) seldom survive in captivity and should never be taken from the reefs.

18. Fish in deep water are not this color.

 a) black

 b) red

 c) grey

 d) beige

19. Triggerfishes, family Balistidae, are aggressive toward other fish and, for the most part, should be kept by themselves or in large tanks with other large fish.

 a) True, triggerfish are curious and opportunistic carnivores that will feed on any animal smaller then themselves.

 b) False, triggerfish are herbivores and feed, like tangs, on algae present around the reef.

 c) True, even when not protecting a spawn, triggerfish are very territorial and will attack any fish of any species that enters its territory.

 d) False, triggerfish are shy and hide in the reefs when any large fish approaches.

20. A fish that is euryhaline

 a) is always found in freshwater.

 b) is always found in saltwater.

 c) is never found in brackish water.

 d) can withstand great changes in salinity.

17. d) Obligate cleaner fish like the cleaner wrasses feed only on parasites picked from larger fish and seldom survive long in captivity.

18. b) Ha, a trick question. Sure a lot of fish taken in deep water are red when they are brought to the surface, but when they are **in** deep water under natural light they are dark brown or black because red light does not penetrate water for more than about 30 feet. OK, so I have never heard of a beige fish either, but there are light gray, brownish colored fish, which is called beige, I believe.

19. a) The triggerfishes, protected by strong spines and scales so hard and plate-like that they are also called leatherjackets, have very few predators and will eat almost anything that moves. They make very interesting aquarium fish and, almost like terrestrial pets, can develop a special relationship with their aquarist. In nature, triggerfish species that produce benthic eggs, agressively protect their spawn and in some species, males protect the territory of their harem from other males. Most triggerfish, however, range widely and are not particularly territorial when not actively spawning. In captivity, they tend to be aggressive toward other fish in the tank, especially smaller fish, and also nip frequently at invertebrates.

20. d) Many fish, mostly coastal species, can change the way they control the internal regulation of the salt content in their blood and body tissues, and can easily move between salt and freshwater environments, a condition know as euryhalinity.

21. What is usually the most important factor in who wins a battle for territory?

  a) Who is the largest fish.

  b) Who was there first.

  c) Who has the brightest colors.

  d) Who has the sharpest spines.

22. Pelagic fish eggs float because they contain one or more tiny oil droplets.

  a) True, the oil provides boyancy to the eggs and prolarvae.

  b) False, the oil only provides a high energy food source to the developing embryo.

  c) False, fish eggs get their buoyancy from a tiny air bubble, not oil, and this becomes the air bladder in the larval fish.

  d) True, the oil droplet increases in size as the embryo becomes larger.

23. Randall's shrimp goby, *Amblyeleotris randalli*, is one of the most spectacular of gobies because

  a) it is one of the largest of the gobies.

  b) its coloration is unique and striking.

  c) they engage in elaborate courtship displays.

  d) they stand on their tails and dance.

24. What is one of the major characteristics of fishes in the family Gobiidae?

  a) They are all very small fish.

  b) There are only a few species.

  c) The pelvic fins are united and usually form a sucking disc.

  d) They are all herbivorous.

21. b) Unless the intruder is far larger than the resident territorial fish, the resident fish always seems to have the edge in winning battles over territory. Attitude is everything in the fish world.

22. a) The oil droplets in pelagic (free floating) eggs give the eggs and the early larvae (the prolarvae) the buoyancy they need to remain in the upper water strata where they will feed on plankton when the eyes and organ sytems are sufficiently developed- about three days after hatch. The oil droplet is used after the yolk is asorbed and gradually gets smaller as the larva matures. Many larval fish develop an air bladder with a small air bubble during late larval development, but there is no air bubble in a pelagic fish egg.

23. b) Randall's shrimp goby is unique among the watchman or shrimp gobies because of its bright yellow bars and strong dark ocellus at the base of the high dorsal fin.

24. c) The gobies are perhaps the most numerous species of fish in tropical seas and are usually small fish, although some species are of moderate size (the marbled sleeper can reach 26 inches in length). One of the most typical characteristics of gobies is that the pelvic fins are united and form a sucking disc that the gobies use to hold on to the substrate. Most gobies are carnivorous.

25. What are the best foods for marine predatory fish?

a) feeder fish like goldfish and guppies

b) frozen marine shrimp, squid, and clams

c) dry foods specially compounded for marine fish

d) fresh, and live if possible, shrimp, squid and clams

26. Groupers are

a) protogynous hermaphrodites.

b) suitable for community tanks with small fishes.

c) all small predatory fish.

d) closely related to the freshwater bass.

27. The beautiful fire gobies, family Microdesmidae, swim in groups just above the reef. How do they spawn?

a) They scatter their eggs over the bottom at sundown.

b) They are mouthbrooders.

c) They build a burrow in the sand under a rock.

d) They produce live young, the only livebearing goby.

28. Which is the most feared poisonous marine fish?

a) the great white shark.

b) the stonefish.

c) the piranha.

d) the lionfish.

25. b) The best food for predatory marine fish, in my opinion, are frozen foods of marine animal origin. There is a small chance of introducing parasites and disease when feeding fresh foods. The fats in fresh water and terrestrial foods are not good for marine fish. Some commercial dry foods are OK, but they are not "best".

26. a) Groupers are members of the large family Serranidae, the sea basses, and are in a separate family from the freshwater basses, the Centrarchidae. There are several types of hermaphroditism in the Serranidae, but the groupers, *Epinephelus* and *Mycteroperca*, are first female and then male, a condition known as protogynous ("proto", first: "gynous" female) hermaphroditism.

27. c) The firefish, like their close cousins the gobies, spawn by placing a clutch of eggs in a protected burrow.

28. b) The stonefish, *Synanceia verrucosa*, one of the scorpionfishes found in the Indo-Pacific, has extremely poisonous dorsal spines that can cause death if the fish is stepped on in shallow water. This species, like most scorpionfish, depends on camouflage to hide it from predators and prey, thus it does not flee from the hand or foot of a careless human. The great white shark, although it is a feared top level predator that can, and does, attack humans, is not poisonous. The lionfish also has poisonous spines but not as virulent as the stonefish. And the piranha, of course, is a freshwater fish.

29. Clownfish are able to live within the stinging tentacles of anemones because

   a) the anemone recognizes them as friends.

   b) clownfish can never be stung by anemones.

   c) the mucus on the skin of clownfish prevents the anemone from stinging the fish.

   d) as long it is not hungry, the anemone will not sting the clownfish; this is why clownfish sometimes feed the anemone.

30. Which fish is easy to keep in a marine aquarium and is a good species for a beginning aquarist?

   a) Royal gramma, *Gramma loreto*

   b) Moorish idol, *Zanclus cornutus*

   c) Rock beauty angelfish, *Holacanthus tricolor*

   d) Batfish, *Platax pinnatus*

31. The flashlight fish, *Photoblepharon palpebratus*, have a large light organ under their eye.

   a) It contains a culture of luminous bacteria.

   b) They can turn this light off and on by covering it with a flap of skin.

   c) They feed on small crustaceans, mostly copepods.

   d) All of the above are correct.

32. In the marine world, a butterfly is

   a) when someone throws the butter dish across the galley of the boat.

   b) an insect with beautiful wings.

   c) a member of the family Pomacanthidae.

   d) a member of the family Chaetodontidae.

29. c) Young clownfish that have never touched an anemone, or older clownfish that have been separated from an anemone for a long time, can be stung by an anemone. After a few stings and a few hours, the new mucus produced by the clown fish prevents the anemone from discharging its stinging cells.

30. a) Of this group, only the royal gramma is an easy fish to keep. Even though the other three are very well known and their pictures grace the pages of many books and posters, they are usually difficult if not impossible to keep for long in home aquaria. It is very important for aquarists to "do their homework" and only buy fish that they know can be maintained in a home aquarium.

31. d) Public aquariums often display flashlight fish in darkened tanks where they amaze visitors with a show of blinking lights.

32. d) The butterflyfishes, beautiful and delicate reef fishes, are now classified in their own family, the Chaetodontidae. The marine angelfish, Pomacantidae, were once classified with the butterflyfish, but are now in a separate family. Oh sure, b) is also almost correct, but this is an aquarium quiz book, not an insect book. Actually a) is also technically correct, but if you see this often it is time for counseling.

33. What is an important charteristic of the juvenile Atlantic queen angel, *Holocanthus ciliaris*?

a) It looks very much like a miniature adult.

b) It is difficult to keep in a small aquarium.

c) It gets along well with other small queen angels.

d) It feeds on algae and small crustaceans.

34. The Maroon clownfish, *Premnas biaculeatus*,

a) is a gentle species. They never fight.

b) can be kept together in large numbers if they are tank raised juveniles.

c) spawn in groups of three and four.

d) males grow larger than females.

35. The large larvae of tank raised clownfish make them easier to raise than the small larvae from wild caught pairs.

a) True, a lucky mutation has resulted in larger larvae in tank reared clownfish.

b) False, even though tank raised clownfish may be easier to spawn than wild caught fish, there has been no change in the size of the larvae.

c) True, careful selective breeding has increased the average size of the larvae.

d) False, both large tank reared and small wild clownfish larvae are equally as difficult, or as easy, to rear in captivity.

36. The sargassumfish, *Histrio histrio*,

a) feeds on floating sargassum weed.

b) is a good fish for the community aquarium.

c) is the only pelagic frogfish.

d) is a pretty yellow color and is easily seen in the sargassum weed.

33. d) Although the wild diet of adult queen angelfish consists almost entirely of sponges, juveniles feed on algae, reef detritus and small crustaceans. Single specimens can do very well in relatively small aquariums.

34. b) A rather difficult question. If **a)** is wrong, then why is **b)** the correct answer? Maroon clowns are perhaps the most aggressive of the clownfish, a large female will almost always attack and kill any other medium or large maroon clown in its tank. Usually only the smallest males can pair with a large female. Tank reared juvenile maroons are very aggressive toward each other, but when kept in large numbers, the aggression is displaced among many targets; no one individual is the object of unrelenting aggression, thus all can survive.

35. b) There have been a few rare true mutations in tank raised clownfish, but very few, and larger larval size is not one of them. Some well fed clownfish pairs produce larvae that seem larger and healthier than other pairs, but this is more a function of nurture rather than genetics. Healthy larvae from well nourished parents all tend to be the same size from both wild and tank reared parents of the same species.

36. c) Sort of a trick question. The sargassum weed is pelagic and the sargassumfish lives in the floating weed and goes along for the ride. They are voracious predators, easily taking fish that are almost as large as themselves, and are so well concealed in the sargassum weed that they are almost impossible to see.

37. What is the composition of the world wide family of marine angelfishes, Pomacanthidae?

a) seven genera and 74 species

b) ten genera and 112 species

c) fifty genera and 35 species

d) twenty genera and 30 species

38. The raccoon butterflyfish, *Chaetodon lunula*, is unusual because it is

a) active during the night, unlike other butterflyfish.

b) one of the few butterfly fish with an "eye mask".

c) known to wash its food before eating.

d) found in brackish water.

39. Hagfish tie themselves in a knot to help them

a) feed on the bodies of dead whales.

b) escape from predators.

c) get rid of excess mucus.

d) do all of the above.

40. Pearlfish, *Carapus bermudensis*, find refuge inside the holothurian (sea cucumber) *Actinopyga agassizi*, and enter the sea cucumber's anus, tail first.

a) False, Oh come on - This can't be true, a pearlfish, *Carapus* ?, going tail first into the anus of a sea cucumber? You expect us to believe that?

b) True, pearlfish really like sea cucumbers.

c) False, the pearlfish actually lives in the sand beneath the sea cucumber and doesn't really enter the sea cucumber, although this may appear true.

d) True, the essential need for protection from predators has driven fish species to evolve many unique ways to find protective shelter.

37. a) According to Fishes of the World, 2nd Edition, by Joseph. Nelson, there are seven genera and 74 species of marine angelfish. If you guessed **c)**, go to the back of the class because there can't be more genera than there are species.

38. a) The scientific name of the raccoon butterfly fish, *Chaetodon lunula*, offers a clue to the correct answer. This species is usually active at night rather than during daylight. Most butterfly fish conceal the location of their eye with a band of dark color, which serves to "hide" their head from predators.

39. d) The primitive hagfish or slime eels live on the deep ocean bottom and scavenge much of their food from dead fish and marine mammals. They can tie their long bodies into an overhand knot and slide this knot down their body from front to rear. This process is thought to help them feed, avoid predation, and rid them of excess mucus.

40. d) Yes it's quite true. The pearlfish first finds the anus of the sea cucumber with its head end and then bends its slender body into a U shape, inserts it sharp tail into the sea cucumber, and wiggles backward until it is entirely within the sea cucumber. The sea cucumber doesn't seem to mind at all.

41. In nature, all species of clownfish

   a) associate with any type of nearby anemone.

   b) are able to survive quite well without an anemone.

   c) for the most part, are rather specific in their choice of host anemones.

   d) associate with various corals as well as anemones

42. Sharks cannot be kept in home aquariums.

   a) True, sharks must keep swimming to breathe and need large areas to swim.

   b) False, there are some small species of sharks that are slow moving and can survive and reproduce in an aquarium if their special needs are met.

   c) True, the large size of sharks prevents them from living in aquariums.

   d) False, sharks will eat almost anything, which makes them easy to keep.

43. The beautiful purple fire goby, *Nemateleotris decora*,

   a) is found swimming above the reef feeding on zooplankton.

   b) lives in a burrow near the reef.

   c) is actually in the family Microdesmidae and is not a goby at all.

   d) is all of the above.

44. What butterflyfish, family Chaetodontidae, are not found in pairs?

   a) the bannerfishes, *Heniochus* spp.

   b) the Red Sea raccoon, *Chaetodon fasciatus*

   c) the butterflyfishes in the genus *Forcipiger*

   d) all species, except during the spawning season

41. c) Clownfish are rather specific in their choice of anemones although some have several specific choices--ten different species in the case of *A. Clarkii.* Others, such as *A. sebae,* occupy only one species of anemone. All clownfish associate with anemones in nature, but in captivity, clownfish may also associate with varioius other species of coelentrates.

42. b) A home aquarist can successfully keep several species of sharks, such as the wobbegongs, *Orectolobus,* epaulett sharks, *Hemiscyllium,* and bamboo sharks, *Chiloscyllium.* Juvenile nurse sharks, *Ginglymostoma cirratum,* also do well in captivity but soon outgrow most home aquariums. An aquarist who wants a shark must make a strong commitment to gaining knowledge and providing for the needs of these fish before taking on the task of keeping a healthy shark.

43. d) The classification of these most beautiful of small reef fish is still not completely understood, but most ichthyologists place them in a family separate from the gobies, even though they are generally considered to be among the gobies.

44. a) Butterfly fish are usually found in pairs and seldom in schools. Bannerfish in the genera *Heniochus* and *Hemitaurichthys,* however, are almost always in schools. There are some more typical species of butterfly fish that also school, such as the double-saddle butterfly and the barberfish. Schooling species usually feed on zooplankton and the schooling habit offers protection from predators.

45. Why might waving white lines be attractive to reef fish?

a) They indicate that a reef is nearby.

b) They advertise relief from parasites.

c) They mark a temperature change in the water.

d) They are a signal that food organisms are present.

46. *Anthias* **are**

a) a popular aquarium fish and members of the sea bass family Grammidae.

b) a small and not well known species of marine ants that are sometimes found around bits of food dropped on the tops of marine aquariums

c) a good fish for small tanks and beginning aquarists.

d) a good example of protogynous hermaphroditism in serranid fishes.

47. How many fins does the "typical" fish have?

a) 5: the dorsal, caudal, anal, pelvic, and pectoral

b) 8: the spiny dorsal, soft dorsal, caudal, anal, 2 pelvic and 2 pectoral

c) 7: the dorsal, caudal, anal, 2 pelvic, and 2 pectoral

d) This is a stupid question because there is no "typical" fish.

48. Why is the coris wrasse, *Coris gaimard*, a favorite of reef aquarists?

a) They are always in the water column and add beauty and movement to the reef.

b) They feed on small snails that often parasitize *Tridacna* clams.

c) They live in little red holes in the substrate.

d) They reproduce easily in a reef tank.

45. b) Parasite picking shrimp of many species have long white antennae. They typically stand at the edge of a coral head or rock and wave their antennae to attract fish to their cleaning station.

46. d) This could be a tough question for you. You could think that a) is correct because it sounds right except that *Anthias* is a genus in the sea bass family Serranidae and not a member of the basslet family, Grammidae. You have to know your taxonomy to eliminate a). And *Anthias*, although a genus of beautiful fish popular in public aquariums, are not well suited for small tanks and beginning aquarists. Protogynous hermaphroditism is a form of sequential hermaphroditism where an individual fish is first a female and then becomes a male as it ages, a form of intersexuality common in fish of the sea bass family Serranidae.

47. c) OK, so for you get the right answer to this question, your opinion has to be the same as mine, which is that the typical fish has 7 fins. Although, sharks have 8, most lungfish have 5, and the salmonids, with their cute little adipose fin, also have 8. And if the dorsal fin is really split into separate spiny and soft dorsal fins like the cardinalfishes and the goatfishes, then there are also 8 fins. But "typical" fish like the snappers, grunts and angelfishes have 7. Barb says you should also get credit if you picked d).

48. b) The coris wrasse and the six-line wrasse, *Pseudocheilinus hexataenia*, are peaceful wrasses and do the reef aquarist a big favor by removing tiny clam eating snails.

49. What is the most important factor for captive propagation of marne fish?

a) They require certain foods before they will spawn.

b) The larvae are very small and require a very small first food organism.

c) They need a great deal of natural area before they can be brought to spawning condition.

d) Their requirement for high water quality exceeds what can be achieved in small aquarium systems.

50. Which is the most important thing to provide for yellowhead jawfish, *Ophistognathus aurifrons*, in an aquarium?

a) adequate lighting

b) small floating food particles

c) at least four inches of sand, rock and shell substrate

d) several companion jawfish

51. Why does a territorial fish display aggressive behavior?

a) It is protecting a food supply.

b) It is guarding eggs.

c) It is maintaining possession of a choice shelter.

d) All of the above

52. This is a good example of a fish that is a microcarnivore.

a) the seahorses, family Syngnatidae

b) the larval stage of the marine angelfish, family Pomacanthidae

c) the moray eels, family Muraenidae

d) the scorpionfish, family Scorpaenidae

49. b) Although there are many and varied reasons for an aquarist's lack of success in propagating marine fish, perhaps the greatest is the need for a suitable first food organism. Rotifers fill this need for many species, but the aquarist must culture adequate stocks of these tiny organisms.

50. c) Actually all of these things are important for the health and comfort of jawfish, but without adequate substrate to build their burrows, yellowhead jawfish will quickly die from stress or jump from the tank.

51. d) There can be a number of reasons for aggressive behavior in territorial fish but reproduction, food, and shelter are the most common.

52. a) Microcarnivores feed on very small animal organisms. In order for seahorses and mandarin fish to find enough food, the tank must be rich in small crustaceans like copepods and amphipods and other tiny organisms. OK, you get half credit for answer b). Technically larval fish feed on microorganisms, but they are microorganisms themselves, what else would they feed on?

53. Ctenoid scales make a fish rough to the touch and

    a) are found on sharks.

    b) are found on all fish.

    c) are on all fish except sharks.

    d) are on most of the spiny rayed fishes like the sea basses and butterflyfishes.

54. In all flatfishes, the right eye in the larval fish migrates around the head and becomes fixed on the left side of the fish.

    a) False, the eyes are in the proper place when the larva hatches from the egg.

    b) True, this is a developmental stage of all flatfish.

    c) True, but sometimes the right eye moves around before hatching occurs.

    d) False, not only does the left eye sometime move around the head, in some species one eye moves through the head to finally appear on the same side as the other eye.

55. The turkeyfish, *Pterois volitans*,

    a) is often served in late November.

    b) is a predator with long, sharp, poisonous spines.

    c) under stress, makes a noise like a wild turkey.

    d) is found only in the far eastern Mediterranean Sea, off Turkey.

56. Where do you find fish with very large eyes?

    a) in very deep water

    b) in caves and deep within the reef structures

    c) feeding at night

    d) all of the above

53. d) Ctenoid scales are mostly large and flat with tiny teeth on the outer edge that give the fish a very rough texture when rubbed from tail to head. These tiny teeth may function to improve swimming efficiency. Cycloid scales are smooth without tiny teeth and are found on fish like trout and herrings. Sharks also feel rough to the touch, but this is caused by placoid scales that have "denticles", small enamel covered spines that protrude above the skin which give the shark its very rough and abrasive surface. Shagreen is the cured skin of certain sharks and is used as a fine abrasive for sanding and processing wood and other materials.

54. d) Another tricky question. There are many families and subfamiles of flatfish: left eyed flounders, right eyed flounders, soles, and toungsoles are the major ones; and although all have a developmental process that finishes with both eyes on one side, the migrating eye may travel various paths depending on the species.

55. b) Turkeyfish is another name for lionfish, a popular group of scorpionfishes, family Scorpaenidae. The scorpionfish get their name from their very poisonous dorsal spines and the turkyfish may get this common name because, when threatened, they spread their very long spined pectoral fins into a large fan, not unlike the fully spread, tail feather display of the male turkey.

56. d) Large eyes indicate that the fish functions best in conditions of low light so this adaptation is found in both deepwater and night feeding fishes.

57. A facultative cleaner fish, like the neon goby, *Gobiosoma oceanops,*

  a) is an excellent addition to a marine aquarium.

  b) should be fed only live food.

  c) seldom survives in captivity and should never be taken from the reefs.

  d) does best in groups of 5 to 8 individuals.

58. Why are fishes of the family Balistidae known as triggerfishes?

  a) They respond aggressively to other fish and are "quick on the trigger".

  b) They have an actual trigger spine.

  c) They were initially described by Count Triggerodsky in the 17 century.

  d) Their large movable pelvic bone is triggered to extend a ventral flap as a defense mechanism.

59. The candy basslet, *Liopropoma carmabi,*

  a) is a rare deepwater species from the tropical Atlantic.

  b) looks like a piece of striped candy.

  c) is very shy and reclusive.

  d) is all of the above.

60. What is the function of the lateral line of a fish, a series of small pores along its side?

  a) to "smell" the water to detect the presence of other fish

  b) to produce mucus that guards the skin of the fish

  c) to provide a *ferntastsinn* sense

  d) to do all of the above

57. a) Unlike obligate cleaners, facultative cleaners like the neon goby can feed on many things besides parasites picked from larger fish. Their cleaner fish feeding mode, however, as well as their bright color makes them very desirable aquarium fish.

58. b) Unique among fishes, when the large and strong first spine of the triggerfish's dorsal fin is erected, the small second spine moves forward and locks the first spine in place. The strong first spine then cannot be depressed unless the triggerfish first moves the second spine out of the locked position. This makes the fish very hard for a predator to swallow and also allows the triggerfish to lock itself into a small cavity in the reef at night or when a predator approaches.

59. d) Although the candy basslet is a good aquarium fish, it is rarely found in the trade because of its deep water habitat and shy nature.

60. c) The *ferntastsinn* sense is a sense of "distant touch" and provides the fish with a way to feel the waves of water movement generated from nearby and distant movement in the water. Thus schooling fish can sense the movement of other fish in the school and predatory fish can sense the movements of prey organisms. These pores contain cells that are mechanoreceptors, not chemoreceptors, thus they do not detect "smells" in the water.

61. What is the reproductive mode of the small bass like dottybacks, family Pseudochromidae?

    a) mouthbrooding by the male

    b) production of a patch of eggs attached to the substrate and guarded by the female

    c) an egg ball deposited in a den by the female and guarded by the male

    d) a large number of small eggs released in the open water by the female and fertilized by the male

62. Why do most newly hatched larval fish move toward the surface of the sea?

    a) This brings them to the plankton rich upper water column where they can find food.

    b) They are better able to avoid the myriad plankton feeding animals on the reefs below.

    c) The surface currents move them to areas where they can survive when they become juveniles.

    d) All of the above reasons are correct.

63. The jackknife fish, with it's spectacular dorsal fin, is a member of

    a) the sea bass family, Serranidae.

    b) the drum family, Sciaenidae.

    c) the butterflyfish family, Chaetodontidae.

    d) the AARP.

64. Which fish is the closest relative of the beautiful yellow and purple royal gramma, *Gramma loreto* ?

    a) the beautiful yellow and purple bicolor dottyback

    b) the sea basses of the family Serranidae

    c) the blackcap basslet

    d) the orchid dottyback

61. c) The male prepares and defends an enclosed den and induces a female to deposit her eggs in this den. The male guards the eggs until they hatch in about 6 to 8 days. Much more information on spawning and rearing the orchid dottyback can be found in my book *Breeding the Orchid Dottyback: An Aquarist's Journal.*

62. d) The tiny pelagic larvae of most marine fish can survive only in the upper reaches of the sea for these, and many other reasons. The period of larval life for most of these fish is about three weeks.

63. b) The drum family, Sciaenidae, includes mostly inshore fishes like the drums, croakers, whitings, and sea trouts, but it also includes the reef drums, *Equetus* sp., the hi hat, the spotted drum, and the jackknife fish, all beautiful Atlantic reef fish. Fish, incidently, do not retire, they work until the very end.

64. c) The blackcap basslet, *Gramma melacara*, is in the same genus as the royal gramma and is the most closely related of this group. Even though the coloration of the bicolor dottyback is very similar to the royal gramma, this is an example of convergent evolution and they are not so closely related.

65. The mandarinfishes, *Synchiropus* spp., are easy to keep and are excellent aquarium fish.

a) False, mandarinfish often starve in aquariums.

b) True, mandarinfish do well in established reef tanks.

c) Both of the above are correct.

d) All of the above are incorrect.

66. The flasher wrasses, *Paracheilinus* spp., got their common name from

a) their resemblance to flashlight fish.

b) the quick darting swimming movements of the females.

c) the little raincoats that the males wear.

d) the dorsal fin extensions and color intensity displays of the male.

67. What is an endemic fish?

a) a fish in the family Endemidae

b) a fish that is found only in a specific region

c) a fish that is about ready to spawn

d) a fish that is spreading disease

68. Why are the neon goby, *Gobiosoma oceanops*, a favorite of marine aquarists?

a) A small school of neon gobies make a beautiful display.

b) They eat algae and help keep the tank clean.

c) They sing songs when you put your ear to the side of the tank.

d) They are cleaner fish and pick parasites off larger fish.

65. c) Although apparently contradictory, both statements are correct. The spectacular mandarinfishes are easy to keep in a tank with a large population of tiny crustaceans, such as a well established reef tank, but without this food source, they are doomed to starvation. This often happened before the development of reef tanks, when they were placed in fish tanks without well established microfaunas.

66. d) The relatively deepwater flasher wrasses, also known as filament wrasses or percy wrasses, are known for the beautiful color displays of the males.

67. b) The term endemic refers to a fish or other organism that is found only in a relatively restricted area. For example, 24.3% of the fishes of Hawaii are found nowhere else in the world and are endemic to Hawaii.

68. d) In nature, a pair of neon gobies occupy a prominent location, a "cleaning station", on a large coral head and picks the parasites from groupers and other large fish that come to be cleaned. This cleaning behavior can also be seen in the aquarium. It is seldom possible to keep more than one pair in a typical marine aquarium, although large numbers can be kept in a single hatchery grow-out tank. Sing a song? - highly unlikely.

69. Why are fishes of the family Acanthuridae known as surgeonfishes?

   a) They have medicinal qualities.

   b) There are scalpel-like spines on either side of their caudal peduncle.

   c) In the juvenile stage, they remove parasitic growths and external tumors from other fishes.

   d) They were named after a famous surgeon, Dr. Acanthur.

70. The yellow long-nosed butterflyfish, *Forcipiger flavissimus*, with its beautiful coloration and intriguing long snout is

   a) very difficult to keep in an aquarium.

   b) despite its delicate appearance, easy to keep and a good aquarium fish.

   c) an excellent butterflyfish for all reef aquariums.

   d) a butterflyfish that is easy to breed in captivity.

71. Why is the cardinalfish, *Apogon ellioti*, so very unusual?

   a) It lives inside the mantle of the queen conch.

   b) It is very large for a cardinalfish, over a foot long.

   c) It is not a mouthbrooder.

   d) It has lights inside its digestive track.

72. Which organism surrounds itself with a "blanket" of mucus each night?

   a) the giant clams of the genus *Tridacna*

   b) parrotfish and some of the flasher wrasses

   c) the female octopus when brooding eggs

   d) most fish that spend the night tucked away deep in the coral reef

69. b) Surgeonfish, including tangs and doctorfish, have sharp spines at the base of the tail on the caudal peduncle (some are retractable) that are used defensively. These spines can cause nasty cuts on other fish and on careless humans, hence the common name surgeonfish.

70. b) The yellow long-nosed butterflyfish and its sister species, *F. longirostris*, the black or big long-nosed butterflyfish, are relatively easy to keep in moderate to large aquaria and can even be kept in some reef tanks that have few hard corals.

71. d) Didn't expect this answer did you? *A. ellioti* is from the Gulf of Tongking and has three luminous glandular organs in the digestive track with structures that look like a reflector and a lens all facing inward. The function of these organs is unknown. The cardinalfish that lives in the mantle of the queen conch is *Astrapogon stellatus*, and it stays inside the conch during the day, coming out only at night to feed.

72. b) Some species of parrotfish and wrasses, although in different families, Scaridae and Labridae, share the characteristic of producing a thick mucus coat around themselves at night which discourages predators that might otherwise find a sleeping fish easy prey. It may take all of 30 minutes to produce the mucus blanket at night and also to dispense with it the following morning.

73. How do clownfish breed?

  a) They produce a spawn of brightly colored eggs that are attached to a substrate.

  b) Like most marine fish they release a large number of tiny, free floating, pelagic eggs.

  c) They are mouthbrooders, the male holds the eggs in his mouth until they hatch.

  d) They are livebearers, the female holds the developing eggs and gives birth to baby fish.

74. Why is the yellow tang, *Zebrasoma flavescens*, so popular an aquarium fish for reef tanks?

  a) It is a brilliant yellow color.

  b) It is a good community fish.

  c) It is an efficient algae eater.

  d) It is easy to feed and is very hardy.

75. What is the natural food of the French angelfish, *Pomacanthus paru*?

  a) planktonic copepods and parasites picked from other fish.

  b) sponges grazed from rocks and reefs.

  c) algae grazed from rocks and reefs.

  d) all of the above.

76. The flame pygmy angelfish, *Centropyge loricula*,

  a) can spawn almost every night and each female can produce 100 to 600 tiny pelagic eggs every night.

  b) can reach a total length of 8 inches.

  c) is a protanderous hermaphrodite.

  d) is the most beautiful fish in the sea.

73. a) Clownfish spawn demersal eggs that are attached to the substrate usually at the base of the host anemone. The female usually spends most of her time guarding the territory around the nest while the male cares for the developing eggs. The eggs hatch in 7 to 10 days, depending on temperature, and the larvae are large and ready to feed on the day of hatch.

74. c) Although the yellow tang is popular for all the above reasons, it is it's ability to graze algae in a reef tank that makes reef aquarists praise it.

75. d) All are true when the entire life cycle of the French angelfish is included. Juvenile French angelfish are parasite pickers and will clean larger fish that visit their territory. They also pick copepods and other organisms from the zooplankton. As adults, their diet is composed mainly of sponges (about 75%) and algae (about 15 %) grazed from the reef environment.

76. a) Well nourished pigmy angels spawn readily in relatively small tanks and can produce hundreds of tiny eggs each night that are only half a millimeter in diameter. They only reach about 4 inches total length, however, and are **protogynous** hermaphrodites (female to male). Some might say that d) is also correct, but this is a matter of opinion.

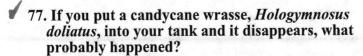

77. If you put a candycane wrasse, *Hologymnosus doliatus*, **into your tank and it disappears, what probably happened?**

   a) It was eaten by another fish, since small wrasses are prey for many fish.

   b) It buried itself completely in the sand and may not come out for days.

   c) It could not take the stress of transport, hid deep in the rocks and died there.

   d) The tank was not covered and it jumped from the tank.

78. Why is the goby *Trimmatom nanus* **unique?**

   a) The adult is shorter in length than it's scientific name.

   b) It is the only goby that has a lateral line organ.

   c) It is parasitic inside the blow holes of whales.

   d) It is harvested for its liver which is thought to be an aphrodisiac.

79. If you had the most fecund fish in the sea, which of these fish would you have?

   a) a white shark

   b) a *Mola mola*

   c) a moray eel

   d) the California giant sea bass

80. This is an example of a fish that has no bones.

   a) a jellyfish

   b) a tuna fish

   c) a tiger shark

   d) a neon goby

77. b) Although all of the choices are possibities, most small wrasses have the habit of burying themselves completely in a sandy substrate at night or when danger threatens. So these small colorful and, for the most part, good aquarium fish must be given a sandy bottom in order to lead happy and stress free lives in a marine tank.

78. a) The goby *Trimmatom nanus*, at a total length of ½ inch, is the smallest fish (actually the smallest adult vertebrate) in the world. It lives on the coral reefs of the western Pacific. (Don't send us any comments about teeny tiny type.)

79. b) This is a tricky question, first you have to know that fecund means "capable of producing offspring (or fertilized eggs)" and that the ocean sunfish, *Mola mola*, can produce up to 300 million eggs, more than any other fish.

80. c) Yeah, sure, a jellyfish doesn't have any bones, but it isn't a fish either; it's an invertebrate, one of the coelenterates. Unlike the bony fishes, the "skeletons" of cartilaginous fishes, including the Elasmobranchs (sharks and rays), are composed of cartilage without any ossified bone; so sharks do not have "real" bones. The only "hard parts" of the shark that are mineralized are the teeth, which is why fossil shark teeth are common, but other shark fossils are not.

Marine Invertebrates

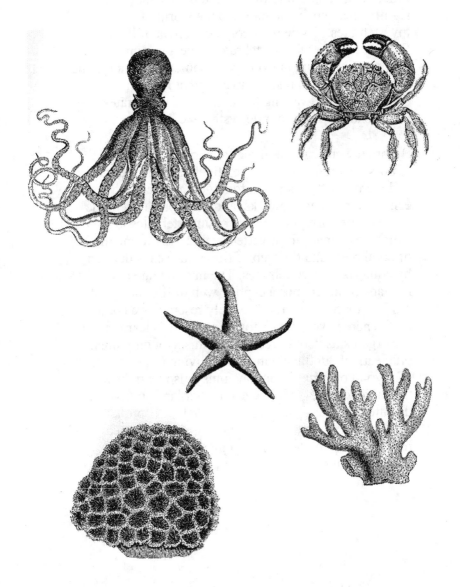

Marine Invertebrates

The vast majority of the animals alive today, and at any point throughout evolutionary history, are invertebrates. Despite the vast distribution and the immense variation in form, function, and structure of the vertebrates, they pale in significance when compared to the world of invertebrates. Of the 92 recognized phyla of life on Earth, 61 phyla of invertebrates have a reasonable chance of showing up someway, sometime, in a marine aquarium. This represents a very great number of organisms, far dwarfing the number of vertebrates that might show up in a marine system.

Before the emergence of reef aquariums in the mid 1980's, invertebrates were relatively rare in aquaria and were mostly restricted to larger crustaceans, echinoderms, and mollusks, and perhaps an anemone or two. The current emphasis on invertebrates is a welcome change; for invertebrates are the foundation of coral reefs and the web of life in the sea is defined by a matrix of invertebrates. The invertebrate core of a reef aquarium creates a captive web of life for the modern marine aquarist that truly resembles a coral reef. There is very much for an aquarist to learn about the organisms kept in reef aquariums. Not only must one learn about the identities and living requirements of myriad organisms, but one must also learn how they live together, combat each other, and survive despite fierce competition and a harsh environment. The following questions should test your knowledge of marine invertebrates, and you may even learn something new.

1. The term invertebrate refers to

    a) all the lower animals.

    b) any animal that does not have a backbone.

    c) all the intracrainates except for the acrainates and the twin brained chordates.

    d) all animals except those in the Phylum Chordata.

2. Why are *Lobophyllia* spp. and other similar species called brain corals?

    a) Only very intelligent aquarists are able to keep them.

    b) They typically grow in large rounded colonies.

    c) They have very large nerve cells, useful in brain and nerve research.

    d) They are all characterized by a surface configuration that resembles the convolutions on the surface of the vertebrate brain.

3. What creates the stunning, gorgeous, glorious colors displayed in the mantle of the giant clams?

    a) the reflection of light from the refractive cells in the mantle tissue

    b) a tiny elf with a great paint brush and a wild imagination

    c) the pigments in the chromatophores of the mantle

    d) the color of the symbiotic algae in the mantle tissue

4. Which of these is characteristic of mushroom corals, *Fungia* spp.?

    a) free living and reproduce with acanthocauli

    b) live in deep waters

    c) soft and flexible and are many colored

    d) require the intense stimulation of wave surge

1. b) The term invertebrate is not an "official" classification in animal taxonomy. It refers, in a general way, to all the non-chordate phyla and the chordates other than vertebrates. In general, an invertebrate is an animal that doesn't have a backbone. This includes the "primitive" chordates, lancelets and tunicates that have a notochord (only in the larval stage for tunicates) but do not have spinal columns protected by bone or cartilage. Separation of animals into "upper" and "lower"classifications is not really meaningful in a biological evolutionary sense, and c) is just gobbledegook

2. d) The term "brain coral" has little specific meaning. Almost any coral of massive structure with a grooved, convoluted surface has been called some type of "brain coral". Typical genera, in addition to *Lobophyllia*, are *Symphyllia, Diploria, Trachyphyllia, Goniastrea, and Platygyra.* Corals are simple animals and do not have "nerve cells".

3. d) Like corals, giant clams maintain symbiotic algae, *zooxanthellae*, within their mantle tissue, and it is these algae that provide the color in the clam's mantle. Oh, yeah, don't tell anyone if you see the elf.

4. a) Mushroom corals should not be confused with the soft bodied mushroom anemones, *Actinodiscus*. Mushroom corals have a stony ridged skeleton and live solitarily on sand or mud bottoms where water movement is slow. Acanthocauli are tiny polyps that develop on the stony skeletons of mushroom corals and then break off and develop into new individuals.

5. The horseshoe crab, *Limulus polyphemus*, often found in marine aquariums, is notable because

   a) it is one of the largest crustaceans.

   b) it is more closely related to spiders than crustaceans.

   c) it is a very recently evolved species.

   d) none of the above.

6. Where is a tube foot found?

   a) clams

   b) crustaceans

   c) nudibranchs

   d) sea urchins *(echinoderms)*

7. The cleaner shrimps of the genus *Lysmata* are

   a) large and aggressive.

   b) small and cryptically colored.

  • **c)** hermaphroditic.

   d) compulsive about keeping their dens clean.

8. In the spider crab family, Majidae, there is a small crab, *Stenocionops furcata*. Why is it called a "decorator" crab?

   a) The shells of this crab are used as decorations in various Asian countries.

   b) In an aquarium, this crab is constantly moving objects around the tank and changing the look of the tank.

   c) The markings on the shell seem to spell out "Kelvin Cline".

   d) The crab collects bits of sponge, anemones, and algae and adheres this matter to the back of it's shell.

5. b) Horseshoe crabs are in the great phylum Arthropoda, but they are not crustaceans (Class or Subphylum Crustacea). They are in the class Merostomata and are more closely related to spiders and other arachnids (Subphylum Chelicerata). They are an ancient line, surviving relatively unchanged for 400 million years.

6. d) All echinoderms, including sea urchins, have a water vascular system that serves to distribute body fluids and to power the locomotor system that moves them about. The tube foot, usually with a suction cup at the end, is the external projection of their water vascular system.

7. c) These small shrimps, 1 to 3 inches long, are favorites of marine aquarists because of their cleaning behavior and bright colors. They wave their long white antennae to attract fish to their cleaning station and then pick the parasites off the sides of the fish. They change sex readily and the female mode occurs after molting.

8. d) There are a lot of crabs, 4,500 species in 47 families, and many have evolved unusual (to us humans) ways to protect and camouflage themselves. The sponge crabs, *Dromidia* spp. have modified rear legs that hold large sponges on their backs and the decorator crabs achieve the same effect by "decorating" themselves with a wide variety of organisms and detritus attached to short hooked hairs (invertebrate "Velcro") that cover their backs.

9. If you have a planula in your reef aquarium then

　　a) you better check your pH.

　　b) at least one of your corals is evidently doing well.

　　c) you may need a deep sand bed.

　　d) you have a species of *Sinularia* in the aquarium.

10. What is a "tabletop" coral?

　　a) a growth of *Acropora* that has reached the surface and spread out horizontally forming a large level surface

　　b) a large coral head that has erroded at the base so that it is growing on a pedestal

　　c) a deepwater coral that grows out from under a ledge

　　d) an ornamental dead coral skeleton that is kept on a table

11. If you have a "turbo" in your tank, you have

　　a) a very fast snail.

　　b) a clam in the genus *Turbo*.

　　c) an efficient protein skimmer.

　　d) a small snail that is an efficient herbivore.

12. The spiny lobsters, *Panulirus* spp., grow large through the process of ecdysis.

　　a) False, like other crustaceans, spiny lobsters grow by molting.

　　b) True, ecdysis (Greek for "getting out") is the scientific term for molting in snakes and crustacea.

　　c) False, spiny lobsters, unlike other crustaceans, grow by gradual extension of the exoskeleton.

　　d) True, only spiny lobsters use ecdysis, the longitudinal splitting of the carapace.

9. b) When corals reproduce sexually, the fertilized egg forms a planula larva, which settles out of the plankton and attaches to a hard substrate. If corals spawn in a reef aquarium, then they are doing very well in their captive environment. Leather corals, *Sinularia* spp. do produce planula larvae when they spawn, but so do other corals. So, if you have planula larvae in your tank, you may have a *Sinularia*, but not necessarily so.

10. a) The term table top refers to the flattened surface of a fast growing *Acropora* that can no longer grow upward and forms a large flat surface. d) may also apply but probably not in reef aquarist circles.

11. d) One of the great tribulations in the life of many reef tank aquarists is the growth of unwanted algae that competes with coral. The small snails in the genera *Turbo, Astraea,* and others do a good job of grazing algae, but there has to be enough of them to be effective. About one per gallon should do the trick. Reduction of phosphate levels is also very important in control of unwanted algae.

12. b) The hard exoskeleton of all crustaceans prevents growth unless this hard outer covering, essential for form and protection, is cast off. A new, flexible exoskeleton forms underneath and when the old one is cast off, the new one expands and then hardens, a process that allows incremental growth. The old exoskeleton splits horizontally across the dorsal surface at the joint between carapace and abdomen. The crustacean then extracts itself from both sections of the old exoskeleton.

13. Sponges survive transport best if

a) they are drained and then shipped in wet paper.

b) they are shipped under pure oxygen.

c) they are always kept under water and never exposed to air when transferred from tank to bag and bag to tank.

d) allowed to empty their gut before packing.

14. If you have a thumb splitter, *Squilla* spp.,

a) you have a nasty algae that will slime up the tank.

b) you are very lucky, these are quite rare.

c) you will probably lose small fish and shrimp.

d) you have the snapping clam, *Hingeous clampii*.

15. What makes *Cassiopea*, the most common jellyfish in the in the marine trade, an unsual jellyfish?

a) They often feed on small fish.

b) Unlike other jellyfish, they avoid bright light.

c) They have a commensal relationship with a small species of octopus.

d) They spend most of their time resting upside down on the bottom.

16. When selecting a blue starfish, *Linckia laevigata* for a marine aquarium, it is important to

a) pick the largest individual.

b) check for tiny clam-like parasites under the arms.

c) make sure that the star has five arms.

d) make sure that the water vascular system is pumping water under high pressure (use the deluxe model of the echinoderm water pressure sensor gauge).

13. c) Sponges are very, very porous (no kidding) and quickly drain water and trap air in their tissues when taken from the water. It is difficult for them to expel these air bubbles, and this often causes their tissues to begin to die and decay. By the way, sponges don't have guts, they are simply an aggregation of several types of cells that form a simple organism.

14. c) The thumb splitter, or mantis shrimp, particularly the Atlantic species, *Squilla empusa*, usually enters a reef tank as a very small juvenile hidden in a deep hole in new live rock. It soon grows large, and with its lighting speed and fierce claws, it begins to feed on small fish and shrimp. They are called thumb splitters because they can give you a nasty cut if you grab one. Catching these predators is often difficult, but entrapment of some type usually works. Come on, you didn't buy that "snapping clam", did you?

15. d) Although most jellyfish are free floating, pelagic creatures, *Cassiopea*, the "upside down" jellyfish, usually rests with the bell of the medusa on shallow, silty bottoms and the short tentacles extending upward. Although it does swim frequently, it is mostly sedentary and adapts to typical aquarium foods, which makes it a jellyfish that can be easily kept.

16. b) The beautiful blue starfish can be any shade from pale blue to intense purple and usually does well in marine aquariums. There is a small parasitic mollusk that sometimes penetrates into the underside of the arms. They can be easily removed, but it is important to check for their presence.

17. **The beautiful, brilliant orange and red** *Dendronephthya* **sp. soft coral is very difficult to keep, probably, in part, because they lack** *zooxanthellae* **.**

   a) False, all soft corals have *zooxanthellae*.

   b) True, they feed on microorganisms, including phytoplankton, instead of harboring *zooxanthellae*.

   c) False, *Dendronephthya*, like its close relative the orange *Tubastrea*, is easy to maintain with intense light.

   d) True, they are found on the reef crest and require high surge conditions.

18. **A snapping or cracking noise in the aquarium is most likely a sign that**

   a) the bottom of the aquarium has just cracked.

   b) a pistol shrimp has found its way into the tank.

   c) a sea urchin has pushed a rock off the reef.

   d) a hermit crab has just changed shells.

19. **In what invertebrate does an aquarist find Aristotle's lantern?**

   a) sea urchins

   b) star fish

   c) sea anemones

   d) barnacles

20. **What is a limpet?**

   a) a very flexible soft coral

   b) a crab in the soft shell stage

   c) a primitive gastropod (a snail)

   d) a type of clam

17. b) The beautiful *Dendronephthya*—so difficult to keep. They have no *zooxanthellae* and their supporting spicules can be seen through their tissues. They can be fed by frequently stirring the bottom to release microorganisms into the tank and/or by frequent additions of planktonic algae. They occur naturally in deep water under ledges and in caves, so intense light is not required. The hard sunflower coral, *Tubastrea*, although similar in color, is a very, very distant relative.

18. b) The pistol or snapping shrimp, family Alpheidae, have an enlarged claw. A small plug on the last segment of this claw fits into a pocket in the preceding segment and when the claw is opened and shut rapidly, a loud snap or pop is created. Small fish or prey organisms in the vicinity are stunned by the sound and are then captured by the shrimp.

19. a) Pliny the Elder (A.D. 23-79) described the mouth parts of sea urchins: five "jaws", each with a single tooth that surround the esophagus, and called this structure Aristotle's lantern.

20. c) There are two Atlantic families of limpets, the Patellacea, and the keyhole limpets, Fissurellacea. (A common Atlantic genus of keyhole limpets is *Diodora* spp.). The shell of a limpet is shaped like a shallow cone, a Chinese hat shape, and the keyhole limpets (volcano shells) have a small hole or vent at the apex of the cone. There are a number of species, some very small and some over an inch in length. They often enter a reef tank riding in the crevices of live rock and can reproduce in the aquarium.

21. What do the giant clams, *Tridacna* spp., and the solitary corals have in common?

a) They both have "stinging cells" (nematocysts).

b) They both occur only in the tropical Pacific.

c) They both rely on the photosynthesis of symbiotic algae.

d) They are both in the Phylum Cnidaria.

22. Anemones often lose color and waste away in aquariums. What is necessary to prevent this loss?

a) intense reef aquarium lighting

b) a feeding of shrimp or fish once a week or so

c) a normal to high calcium content in the water

d) all of the above

23. Fire corals, order Milleporina (thousand pores)

a) are very slow growing.

b) get their name because of their fiery color.

c) have very "hot" nematocysts.

d) develop extensive growths like other stony corals.

24. The boxer or banded coral shrimp are always found as pairs, a large male and a smaller female.

a) True, since the female eventually becomes a male.

b) False, the male is almost always smaller than the female.

c) False, these shrimp occur in groups rather than pairs.

d) True, they mate for life.

21. c) The giant clams and the solitary corals are in vastly different phyla, Mollusca and Cnidaria, but both harbor *zooxanthellae* in their tissues that provide them with energy though the photosynthesis of the algae. Solitary corals are found in tropical waters worldwide, but giant clams are found only in the Indo-Pacific.

22. d) Anemones are not corals, but are very similar. Most have *zooxanthellae* and with the proper lighting they can obtain much of their food from this symbiosis, but most do better with an occasional feeding. Even though they do not have stony skeletons, they require calcium and strontium for basic metabolism.

23. c) The true meaning of the name "fire coral" cannot be understood until one has dragged one's bare belly across the blades of a fire coral reef. Then one knows where the "fire" is in fire coral. Fire corals are not "true" corals, class Anthozoa, but hydrozoans, class Hydrozoa, thus they are not "other stony corals". They do contribute greatly to the reef growth, however, with their rapidly growing, massive formations.

24. b) The banded coral shrimps, 9 (perhaps 10) species of the family Stenopodidae, are not hermaphroditic as are the *Lysmata* shrimps, and always occur in pairs, a small slender male and a robust larger female. The pairs remain together, but if one is lost, the other may form another pair with a new partner.

25. What are the tiny white creatures that are seen on the aquarium glass at night, move in a jerky manner, and are sometimes very abundant?

a) flatworms

b) copepods

c) amphipods

d) coral larvae

26. Cnidaria are

a) stinging cells that are found in corals and anemones.

b) only anemones.

c) carnivores.

d) only corals.

✓**27. The harlequin shrimp, *Hymenocera picta*, are wildly beautiful in form and color. Why are they difficult to keep?**

a) They feed only on starfish and nothing else.

b) They will eventually destroy all other invertebrates.

c) They require a commensal species of coral that is impossible to keep in captivity.

d) They do not do well in shallow water.

28. *Richordea florida* is a beautiful corallimorph found in the Florida Keys and the Caribbean. It gets the specific name *R. florida* from

a) the flower-like appearance of the polyp.

b) its occurrence off the coast of Florida.

c) the discoverer of the species, Herman Florid.

d) the rather florid color of its face.

25. b) There are over 8000 species of copepods and many of these can show up in a marine aquarium. They are a good source of food for a wide variety of reef tank creatures, and their presence is usually good. The white color and jerky movements are characteristic of copepods. Flatworms glide slowly and amphipods are comma shaped.

26. c) Sort of a tricky question, but if you know your invertebrates you should be able to figure it out. First of all, "stinging cells" are cnidocytes that are contained in a capsule called a nematocyst. The phylum Cnidaria includes the Hydrozoa (hydras), the Scyphozoa (true jellyfish), the Anthozoa (corals and anemones), and the Cubozoa (sea wasps), so this eliminates both b) and d). A carnivore is any animal that consumes other animals; and all cnidaria, with their stinging cells and gut (the gastrovascular cavity) have the capability, the opportunity, and perhaps even the requirement, to feed on other animals, mostly small zooplankton. Some Cnidaria apparently survive just on the energy produced by *zooxanthellae*, but their gut is functional and some feeding probably takes place.

27. a) The harlequin shrimp is well named; with its flaps and bright colors, it is very reminiscent of the traditional harlequin clown. The diet is very specialized, however, and even though they adapt well to aquarium conditions, a ready supply of starfish must be available to keep them well fed. A serious aquarist, however, can maintain starfish for these shrimp.

28. b) Sometimes the most obvious answer is the correct one.

29. Brittle stars, starfish, sea urchins and sea cucumbers are all echinoderms and all have what particular characteristics in common?

a) spiny skin, tube feet, and radial symmetry

b) five arms, internal skeletal plates, and a water vascular system

c) an extrudable stomach, tube feet, and a madreporite

d) radial symmetry, slow moving manner, and bright colors

30. Which octopus is most dangerous to people?

a) the blue-ringed octopus, *Hapalochlaena lunulata*

b) the common octopus, *Octopus vulgaris*

c) the giant Pacific octopus, *Octopus dofleini*

d) the tropical Pacific octopus, *Octopus cyaneus*

31. The bright red and orange deep water gorgonians in the genus *Diodogorgia*

a) are found in the Indo-Pacific region.

b) do not contain *zooxanthellae*.

c) must be fed phytoplankton.

d) two of the above are correct, and they are....

32. The "Spanish Dancer" is a glorious example of

a) a nudibranch.

b) a gastropod.

c) a *Hexabranchus*.

d) all of the above.

29. a) A difficult question, all choices are characteristic of some echinoderms, but only a) has characteristics that are present in all echinoderms.

30. a) Octopuses are well known for their intelligence and shyness and are generally not considered at all dangerous (although all of them can bite if handled poorly). The beautiful blue-ringed octopus, however, is sometimes found in the marine ornamental trade and has a venomous bite that can be fatal.

31. d) And the two correct answers are a) and b). These are popular aquarium species and do not require intense lighting since they are not photosynthetic. Unlike the red and orange deepwater corals, *Dendronephthya*, that require phytoplankton feedings, the deepwater gorgonians need meaty foods like brine shrimp and finely ground shrimp and clams.

32. d) An easy question, of course. The fabulous Spanish Dancer, *H. imperialis*, and *H. sanguineus*, are nudibranchs, which is an order in the Class Gastropoda. The nudibranchs (naked gills) are "snails without shells" and many are brilliantly colored, probably to advertise their unpalatability to predators. The bright red and white Spanish dancer swims in a swirl of its fluttering crimson mantle, thus it's common name. Alas, they do not do well in captivity.

33. The pulsing hand is a description of

   a) the major character in a horror movie.

   b) an aquarist who has just grabbed a lionfish.

   c) the soft coral *Anthelia* spp.

   d) the complex growth of *Acropora*.

34. Sponges are in which phylum?

   a) Sponginfera

   b) Porifera

   c) Demospongiae

   d) Spongiidae

35. What is the " crown" of the Christmas tree worm, *Spirobranchus*?

   a) part of the digestive track, a growth of feeding tentacles

   b) gills, a part of the respiratory system

   c) the nervous system because it moves so rapidly

   d) dermal tissue since it is sensitive to touch and not to light

36. Which is a good example of an SPS coral?

   a) the sand polyps, *Zoanthus* spp

   b) the torch coral, *Euphyllia glabrescens*

   c) the staghorn corals, *Acropora* spp

   d) the sun polyp corals, *Tubastrea* spp

33. c) The waving or pulsing hand soft corals in the family Xenidae, including the genera *Anthelia* and *Xenia*, are very popular with aquarists, particularly because of the motion of the tentacles around the stalked polyps. The polyps ceaselessly open and close and are reminiscent of a waving hand.

34. b) If you know that families end in "idae" and classes end in "iae", then you can eliminate c) and d) even though they are legitimate scientific terms. The name Porifera means "bearing pores", and is the correct term.

35. b) The crown of these annelid worms is made up of the radioles (the word means spiral gills) and is used for both respiration and feeding. Brown eye spots on the crown can detect changes in light, and a shadow crossing the crown will stimulate a very rapid retraction. The most common species in aquariums is *S. giganteus,* occurring in a variety of colors on both Atlantic and Pacific reefs.

36. c) An SPS coral is a "Small Polyped Stony" coral, and refers to a coral composed of small individual polyps set into a hard, stony, calcareous skeleton. SPS is an artificial classification and is used mostly by aquarium hobbyists to refer to small polyped corals with a branching or plate-like growth. *Acropora* is one of the most well known of these corals.

37. The sea apple, *Pseudocolochirius axiologus*, is

a) a sea cucumber.

b) not dangerous to fish in aquaria.

c) the fruit of the Brazilian sea kelp.

d) found in small lobster's lunch boxes.

38. This is a decapod crustacean with broad, short, and flattened antennae that hides under rocks and has a phyllosome larval stage.

a) scarlet cleaner shrimp

b) spiny lobster

c) slipper lobster

d) porcelain crab

39. *Acropora* corals grow best

a) when given intense lighting.

b) if they are fed regularly.

c) when placed near the bottom of the tank.

d) all of the above

40. Some species of hermit crabs not only make homes of old snail shells, but they also "keep" anemones.

a) True, they grow small species of anemones for food.

b) False, some hermit crabs may eat anemones but they don't "keep" them.

c) True, they deliberately attach anemones to their snail shell homes for protection.

d) False, hermit crabs are opportunistic shell appropriators and sometimes pick up shells with attached anemones.

37. a) This beautiful sea cucumber is about the size of an apple and is spectacular with red tentacles, yellow tube feet, and red and yellow knobs on a greyish body. Unlike most sea cucumbers, it is a filter feeder, catching micro plankton with its tentacles and then pulling them and the captured plankton into the mouth. It does best in an aged reef tank with no particulate filter. It can, if greatly stressed, discharge its gut tissues and poison a tank, killing fish.

38. c) Only the tropical lobsters in the families Palinuridae (spiny), Synaxidae (coral or furry), and Scyllaridae (slipper) have phyllosome larvae, and only the slipper lobsters have broad flat antennae. They are also called "bulldozer" lobsters because of this characteristic.

39. a) An experienced reef aquarist would not be fooled by d). *Acropora* are among the most difficult to keep of corals since they require very high water quality and intense lighting. They usually occur in the surge zone of wave washed reef crests where the water is active and well aerated and sunlight is intense.

40. c) Some hermit crabs, particularly *Pagurus prideauxi*, maintain small anemones on top of their shells, and when they switch shells, they carefully remove the anemones from the old shells and reattach them to the new shell. The anemone benefits by feeding on the scraps that drift up from the hermit's feeding activity, and the presence of the anemone discourages predators interested in the hermit crab.

41. Why are the boxing crabs, the African *Lybia tessellata* in particular, unusual?

   a) They use anemones for protection.

   b) They engage in battles for territory and use their claws like boxing gloves.

   c) Their carapace is shaped like a box.

   d) They occur in groups and form a box-like formation when threatened by predators.

42. The beautiful elegance coral, *Cataphyllia jardenei*,

   a) is the only species in the genus *Cataphyllia*.

   b) is found on muddy bottoms.

   c) is named after Dr. R. Catala.

   d) is all of the above.

43. Sponges do not have zooxanthellae (algae cells within their tissues), thus do not require intense light.

   a) False, all sponge species have *zooxanthellae*.

   b) True, many species of sponges are found in low light conditions in caves and under ledges.

   c) False, most species are found in shallow waters where sunlight is intense.

   d) Neither completely true nor completely false, a good example of an ambiguous question.

44. An octopus, Order Octopoda, has

   a) the ability to produce many cluches of eggs.

   b) eight arms.

   c) 8 arms and two tentacles.

   d) a small internal shell.

41. a) The boxing crabs, *Lybia* spp. carry an anemone in each claw and threaten any predator that approaches by thrusting these anemones toward it, which makes the crab look as if it is waving boxing gloves. It will not release the anemone until the crab molts and then it sets the anemone carefully aside and picks it up again once molting is complete.

42. d) The spectacular elegance is one of the most popular corals for the reef tank and is considered relatively easy to maintain. It was named after Dr. Rene Catala in 1893 and is usually found in turbid water on muddy, silty bottom.

43. d) Ah, the dangers of generalization. Sponges have been around since the beginning and have evolved intimate relationships with almost all forms of life in the sea. They range from microscopic and parasitic to huge formations that function as small ecosystems in themselves. *Zooxanthellae*, perhaps not the same species as in corals, are common in sponges. Sponges without *zooxanthellae* are also common. Sponges generally do better under low light conditions since in captivity they do not compete well with algae. Probably no reef tank with live rock is without some species of sponge.

44. b) But of course you got this one. The name gives away the answer. Octopoda means eight arms, "octa"— eight, and "poda"–arms. Squid, Order Teuthoidea, have 10 arms, two of which are very long and are usually termed tentacles. The molluscan shell has also become internal in squid (cuttlebone), and is absent in octopus. The female dies after her eggs hatch.

45. Sand polyps, button polyps, gold sea mat, and green star polyps are all examples of zooanthids.

a) True, all little polyps linked together in mats are zooanthids.

b) False, there is no such creature known as gold sea mat.

c) True, common names are now so well established that one can be confidant of a common name identification.

d) False, green star polyps are not zooanthids.

46. What do the feather stars and the basket stars, both echinoderms and relatives of starfish and sea urchins, feed on?

a) detritus

b) algae

c) plankton

d) energy produced by *zooxanthellae*

47. What is a spicule?

a) a tiny sponge

b) a hair-like growth found on crustaceans

c) a structural element of various composition found in the tissues of sponges and some corals

d) the sharp hair-like growths on bristle worms

48. Why is the blue-legged hermit crab, *Clibanarius tricolor*, highly desirable for reef tanks?

a) They are very efficient algae eaters.

b) They pick copepods off the glass.

c) They feed on bristle worms.

d) They keep clams clear of parasites.

45. d) Green star polyps (*Briareum* spp., formerly *Clavularia* sp.) are in the family Tubiporidae and are not closely related to zooanthids, family Zoanthidae even though there is a superficial resemblance. Common names cannot be relied upon to provide an accurate identification. Sure, some of the most well known and distinctive species develop a distinguishing common name, but a common name can seldom positively identify the species.

46. c) These most interesting echinoderms, in very different taxonomic groups, subphylum Crinozoa (sea lilies and feather stars) and subphylum Asterozoa (starfish, brittlestars, and basketstars) feed mostly at night by extending their feathery and netlike arms up into the water currents to catch plankton.

47. c) A spicule is a tiny, needle-like growth composed of calcium carbonate, silica, and/or protein and is found internally in various corals and sponges. They provide skeletal support. The shape and size of the spicule is very important in identification of the species. Bristle worms (Class Polychaeta, meaning many chaeta) have a lot of external hair-like chaeta, and crustaceans have "hairs" and bristles.

48. a) No matter how low the nutrient load, a good reef tank needs a lot of algae eaters, and the blue-legged hermits are about the best. They occupy small shells and can get into small spaces, and are very effective in removing unwanted algae.

49. Asexual reproduction is not common among

a) zoanthids.
b) anemones of the family Stichodactylidae.
c) *Aiptasia* anemones.
d) Corallimropharia.

50. What is a kreisel?

a) an aquarium system for keeping jellyfish
b) a type of cold water anemone
c) the base of a coral reef
d) a food storage cell within a sponge

51. The star polyps, *Clavularia* spp.

a) are very easy to keep and are recommended for the beginning reef aquarist.
b) must be fed frequently to grow well.
c) are found on soft muddy bottoms.
d) require intense light.

52. Animals in the Order Decapoda all share one characteristic that is implied by the name. In one of the following groups, all three are in this very large taxon.

a) octopus, squid, chambered nautilus
b) spiny lobster, anemone shrimp, fiddler crab
c) cleaner shrimp, neon goby, coral banded shrimp
d) sea urchin, sea cucumber, star fish

49. b) Asexual reproduction (reproduction by fission, budding and pedal laceration without sex cells or larval production) is very common among the Cnidaria. Marine aquarists are very familiar with the forms of asexual reproduction that fill their tanks with soft and hard corals. One major exception are the large anemones that host clownfish; although asexual reproduction occurs, it is not commonly observed in these anemones.

50. a) Pelagic jellyfish, such as moon jellies, *Aurelia aurita* and sea nettles, *Chrysaoara fuscescens*, were almost impossible to keep in captivity until a special cylindrical tank called a *kreisel* (after the German word for carousel) was developed at the Monterey Aquarium (based on similar Japanese work) in 1991-92. The cylindrical tank sets up revolving currents that keep the slowly floating jellies away from the tank walls.

51. a) The star polyps, *Clavularia*, grow on hard rubble bottoms in shallow waters, often in heavily turbid, slow flowing waters. They do very well in reef tanks and do not need intense lighting.

52. b) The name Decapoda means "ten legs" and all of the decapod crustaceans have ten legs. So the only group that has three crustaceans is b). The a) group are all mollusks, the d) group are all echinoderms and c) are all cleaners, which, of course, is not a taxonomic grouping.

53. If you have a *Heterocentrotus* sp. then

a) your five year old kid wears tattered dirty clothes and sells pencils on the street corner.

b) you can make a wind chime.

c) you have a critter that feeds on algae and detritus.

d) two of the above are correct, and they are....

54. Which is a rigid, branching, twig-like soft coral?

a) a gorgonian

b) a leather coral

c) an anemone

d) a *Xenia*

55. *Stenorhynchus seticornis* has a rather fantastic shape with long, long legs and a triangular body. What is it?

a) a rare deep sea octopus

b) a huge bristle worm

c) a Caribbean basket star

d) a common arrow crab

56. What is the difference between the feather duster fan worms, Family Sabellidae, and the Christmas tree fan worms, Family Serpulidae?

a) They are in different phyla.

b) Feather duster worms build tubes of sand and Christmas tree worms are embedded in coral rock.

c) One is a bristle worm and one is an annelid worm.

d) One has a spiral crown and one does not.

53. d) Yes, you have a pencil urchin and both b) and c) are correct. There are two species that enter the marine aquarium trade, *H. mammillatus*, the one with the big fat spines, and *H. trigonarius*, with smaller spines. They make interesting marine aquarium specimens, although they can move rocks around. They are also harvested for their spines, which are used to make wind chimes and other ornaments. If a) is also correct for you, it is doubtful that you have enough disposable income for a marine aquarium.

54. a) The gorgonians are the only choice that fully fits the above description, but you could be fooled by *Xenia* if you didn't know that the typical gorgonian is rigid and *Xenia* is flexible.

55. d) Oh come on, use your head, the arrow crab is the only choice that has legs! The arrow crab, with its long legs and long sharp rostrum, is a most delicate creature. It feeds on small worms (bristle worms beware) and is fascinating to watch in a reef tank. Just keep one, however, for they often fight with each other.

56. b) The phylum Annelida (meaning little ring) is a vast phylum of segmented worms of which the class Polychaeta (including the bristle worms and the fan worms) is most well known to marine aquarists. They are both annelids and neither is a bristle worm. Both Christmas tree worms and feather duster fan worms have spiral crowns, but the crown of the Christmas tree worm is elongate and the spiral nature of the crown is more evident.

57. Hermatypic corals are

a) corals that are typical of a hermatype.

b) corals that are hollow.

c) corals that contain algae.

d) corals that have both sexes in one individual.

58. What phylum of marine animals is unique with a structure based in pentamerous symmetry?

a) Ectoprocta (Greek *ektos*, outside: *proktos*, anus)

b) Rotifera (Latin *rota*, wheel; *ferre*, to bear)

c) Echinodermata (Greek *echinos*, sea urchin; *derma*, skin)

d) Cnidaria (Greek *knide*, nettle; *koilos*, hollow; *enteron*, intestine)

59. Which is the easiest of the cleaner shrimps to breed in captivity?

a) the fire or blood shrimp, *Lysmata debelius*

b) the peppermint shrimp, *Lysmata wurdemanni*

c) the scarlet cleaner, *Lysmata amboinesis*

d) the coral banded shrimp, *Stenopus hispidus*

60. If you have too many small, brown *Aiptasia* anemones in your tank which is the best way to remove them?

a) smashing them with hard object

b) using the sea slug *Berghia* to eat them

c) adding the copperband butterflyfish to eat them

d) stroking them with an elegance coral

57. c) Corals are divided into two groups: those that contain *zooxanthellae* (an algae that produces food for the coral) within their tissues are hermatypic, and those that do not are ahermatypic. This is an important distinction for reef tank aquarists as placement of a coral in a tank depends on how much light it requires and this is dependent on the symbiotic algae within its tissues.

58. c) Echinoderms, of course. Pentamerous means five and the radial symmetry of Echinoderms is based on five parts The five sectioned structure is most evident in starfish.

59. b) Most cleaner shrimp are very difficult to breed because the conditions they require in the larval stage and for metamorphosis into the juvenile stage are not well known. Most also have a long larval life, which also makes rearing more difficult. The peppermint shrimp, however, are the easiest of this group to breed. They also feed on *Aiptasia* anemones, a plus for reef tank aquarists.

60. b) There are a number of methods for controlling the proliferation of *Aiptasia*, including b), c) and d). Never smash them because all the little pieces will grow into new *Aiptasia* anemones. They can also be injected with a weak copper solution, calcium hydroxide, or boiling water. Peppermint shrimp will also eat them and other coelenterates as well, so be careful. Although using *Berghia* to feed on them is probably best for a heavy infestation, manual removal may be the easiest way to remove small numbers.

61. Sally Lightfoot is frequently found in aquarium shops. What is she?

   a) a dancing nudibranch

   b) a crab

   c) an octopus

   d) a cleaner shrimp

62. What characterizes bubble corals, *Plerogyra* spp.?

   a) large, bubble-like polyps

   b) a large bulbous purple base that keeps it above bottom mud

   c) grape-like vesicles

   d) an absence of nematocysts

63. The soft tissues of coral polyps originate from

   a) four layers of tissues.

   b) two layers of tissues.

   c) one tissue layer.

   d) three tissue layers.

64. The gorgonian at the aquarium store is

   a) a mean and ugly woman.

   b) that strange grotesque carving squirting water into the garden pond.

   c) a medusa floating in the reef tank.

   d) a soft coral growing in a reef tank.

61. b) Sally Lightfoot, *Grapsus grapsus*, (Atlantic) is one of the spray crabs, family Grapsidae, and she makes a very interesting addition to a marine aquarium. These are the crabs that are seen running rapidly over the rocks and tide pools at low tide. They have bright yellow spots on their legs and I'm not sure if the name "lightfoot" comes from being nimble and fast afoot, or from the "lights" on their legs.

62. c) The bubble or "grape" corals, nominally six species in the genus *Plerogyra*, have vesicles on modified tentacles (not polyps) that expand into large bubbles and give them the appearance of a bunch of grapes. They are relatively easy to keep in a good reef tank, but they are capable of a strong sting (they have powerful nematocysts) so aquarists should take care when handling the bubble corals.

63. b) The tissues of most animals originate from three layers of germ cells: ectoderm, the external layer; endoderm, the internal layer; and mesoderm, the central layer. The tissues of cnidarians, among the simplest of animals, including corals and anemones, originate from only two germ layers, the endoderm and ectoderm and are said to be diploblastic. Other animals with the third germ layer are triploblastic.

64. d) Gorgonians, Order Gorgonacea, are colonies of soft corals that grow in tree-like colonies and can reach heights of several feet. Sea whips, sea plumes, sea fingers and sea fans are common names of various species of gorgonians.

65. Which taxon has a structure known as a madreporite?

a) stony corals order, Scleractinia = Madreporaria.

b) arrow worms, phylum Chaetognatha

c) starfish, class Asteroidae

d) tunicates, class Ascidiacea

66. The eggs of the banded coral shrimp, *Stenopus hispidus*, are

a) yellow.

b) held under the females abdomen for two to three weeks before hatching.

c) released immediately after fertilization by the male.

d) placed in a nest and protected by the male until hatching.

67. The barnacles, Class Cirripedia, with their hard shells and permanent attachment are in the same group of mollusks as the hard shelled limpets.

a) True, limpets and barnacles live in the same intertidal areas.

b) False, barnacles are crustaceans not mollusks.

c) True, barnacles are not mobile like the crustaceans.

d) False, barnacles have legs and can move about.

68. Corallimorpharians, the mushroom anemones, are

a) basically corals with an anemone-like structure.

b) difficult to keep in aquariums.

c) ahermatypic corals.

d) none of the above.

65. c) It's easy to be fooled by a name. A madreporite (mother, porous stone) is the small, sieve-like plate on the dorsal surface of the disk of starfish that is the entrance to the water vascular system of these echinoderms. Madreporaria, now usually known as Scleractinia, is the higher taxon (order) of stony corals.

66. b) The male pursues the female after she molts, chasing her and "hugging" her in his long pincher arms. The female finally allows him to mate and they orient tail to tail. Then both extend their tail-like abdomens upward while the male passes sperm onto the female's swimmerets. The female then passes the dark green eggs from her gonads, located under her carapace, through her oviducts and onto her swimmerets where they are attached and fertilized. She then holds them until they develop and hatch.

67. b) Now while it is true that barnacles have hard "shells", are permanently attached to a substrate, and have "legs", it is also true that they are actually crustaceans, which makes the statement false. The six pairs of thoracic limbs or cirri (filaments) have two long jointed and hairy rami (branches) that rhythmically extend in and out of the shell and capture plankton, but these legs do not function in locomotion.

68. a) Although mushroom anemones resemble sea anemones in shape and form, their anatomy is more similar to stony corals. They do not, however, have the stony skeleton of the Scleractinia corals. They are hermatypic (contain *zooxanthellae*) and are easy to keep in well lit aquraria.

69. Tunicates (Ascidiacea), also known as sea squirts, are acraniate (no brain) chordates and

a) are all hermaphroditic.

b) are all colonial.

c) look like and are constructed like sponges.

d) are seldom found in marine aquaria.

70. *Goniopora*, the flowerpot corals, are difficult to keep.

a) False, many aquarists have kept them for years.

b) True, we don't know exactly why, but flowerpot corals typically do well for a few months and then almost always decline and die.

c) False, only inexperienced reef aquarists have problems with this group.

d) True, only the frequent addition of *Eyorangium*, a rare Pacific algae, will allow them to survive in captivity.

71. Sponges are hardy reef tank animals.

a) False, because they require intense light.

b) True for all, because they can grow in any tank.

c) False, because they almost always die in captivity.

d) True for many, but they require special conditions.

72. What are the requirements for good growths of *Xenia*?

a) intermittent but active currents

b) additions of calcium, iodine, and iron

c) intense, reef aquarium lighting

d) all the above

69. a) They are called sea squirts because many have the ability to contract quickly and squirt water from their excurrent siphon a considerable distance. Although they look superficially like sponges, they are complex organisms, and even have a notochord in the larval stage. They may be solitary or colonial but all are hermaphroditic, producing both male and female gametes. They often enter reef tank systems as hitchhikers on live rock and do well in these tanks if sufficient microplankton is present.

70. b) *Goniopora* are spectacular corals and it's a shame that they do not survive well in most reef tanks. Occasionally one will do well in a particular tank for years, but such success stories are few and far between. Oh yes, beware of *Eyorangium*, a rare alga that can invade human eyeballs and turn the world orange. (Don't believe everything you read.)

71. d) In aquarium systems, sponges require little or no competition from algae, the proper trace element composition, and water with a relatively abundant micororganism component. Given these elements, many sponges will survive and grow in captivity.

72. d) *Xenia*, the pulsing or waving hand soft corals, are very popular reef tank corals. Given the right conditions, they propagate asexually very abundantly and make a wonderful addition to almost every reef aquarium.

73. These invertebrates look like sponges but are in the phylum Chordata, more closely related to fish than sponges, and have a tough, flexible exoskeleton.

a) sea squirts, Tunicata

b) gorgonians, Gorgonaceae

c) anemones, *Radianthus*

d) sun corals, *Tubastrea*

74. In which of the following groups are all three organisms most closely related?

a) giant clam, thorny oyster, queen conch

b) chambered nautilus, cuttlefish, blue-ringed octopus

c) horseshoe crab, arrow crab, porcelain crab

d) red finger sponge, scarlet cleaner shrimp, red-legged hermit crab

75. Which is the soft coral with an internal skeleton made of a proteinaceous material?

a) brain coral

b) gorgonian

c) mushroom coral

d) tube anemone

76. Which of these is a little comma shaped crustacean that lives in rocks or on the bottom of the aquarium?

a) copepod

b) shrimp

c) amphipod

d) mantis shrimp

73. a) All of the above have a relatively tough, flexible exterior, but the tunicates, of course, look somewhat like sponges, but are actually complex animals in the phylum Chordata.

74. b) You may have thought that the a) group was more closely related, but there are two great classes of mollusks represented here, the Pelecypoda (bivalves, clams) and the Gastropoda (univalves, snails). Group b) are also mollusks but all are in a single class, Cephalopoda, (squids, octopods, and nautilids). All of c) are in the phylum Arthropoda, but horseshoe crabs are not decapod crustaceans, subphylum Crustacea, but are in fact more closely related to spiders, which are both in the subphylum Chelicerata. Yeah, all of d) are red, not an important taxonomic characteristic at this level.

75. b) The gorgonians, order Gorgonacea, have an internal "skeleton" made of gorgonin, a protein that may or may not be infused with calcium carbonate, and it is this internal skeleton that allows gorgonians to grow into rigid structures.

76. c) There are many, many species in the subphylum Crustacea, about 39,000 to be almost exact. Amphipods (6000 species) are mostly small free living crustaceans that feed on detritus and algae. The curved (comma shaped) body is characteristic of this group and the ones that commonly inhabit reef tanks are about 1/8 to 1/4 inch (5 mm) long.

77. Which of the following groups has the three most closely related organisms?

  a) blue starfish, feather star, basket star

  b) copepod, amphipod, barnacle

  c) arrow crab, snapping shrimp, spiny lobster

  d) Florida spiny lobster, a panulirid phyllosome, Red Sea painted crayfish

78. Why are Zooanthids very popular additions to reef tanks?

  a) There are many species of various shapes and colors.

  b) They are tolerant of less than optimum water quality.

  c) They reproduce asexually and can form large colonies.

  d) all of the above

79. The only time that *Tridacna* clams are mobile

  a) is in the spawning season when the males migrate to the females.

  b) is in the winter when they move closer to the reef crest in search of more sunlight.

  c) is in the larval stage.

  d) is when they are transported to various shops and hobbyists tanks.

80. What is the principal means of reproduction in the Corallimorpharians?

  a) budding

  b) longitudinal fission

  c) nuclear fission

  d) production of gametes

77. d) You have to know your invertebrates to be sure of this one. a) are all echinoderms, but they are from different major classes within this phylum. b) are all in the subphylum Crustacea, but are also in different classes and not closely related. c) are all in the order Decapoda (decapod crustaceans) but in greatly different families. All of d), however, are in the same genus of spiny lobsters, *Panulirus*, thus they are the most closely related. A phyllosome is a larval spiny lobster. One of the common names of *Panulirus versicolor* is the painted crayfish (also known as the painted lobster).

78. d) Almost any reef tank will support and grow some species of zoanthid. They are found in red, green, blue, yellow, brown, and other colors as well. Few reef tanks are without some species of zooanthid.

79. c) Giant clams cannot move themselves around the reef or tank. In fact their byssal threads, extended from the byssal gland, anchor them firmly in one location. However, in the first larval stage (swimming larvae) they swim by beating cilia and in the next larval stage (foot larvae) they can move about for a couple of weeks while searching for a good location to settle and attach. Being moved about by a human being does not make the clam mobile.

80. b) Although other reproductive modes are found in mushroom anemones, longitudinal fission is most common. Nuclear fission is not common in the corallimorpharians, which is too bad, for if it were, they would be a good power source for electrical energy.

Marine Aquaristics

Marine Aquaristics

This section deals with the practice of marine aquaristics, everything from ammonia to zinc, including both basic and advanced aquarium theory. Like all technologies, marine aquaristics evolves over time, sometimes rapidly and sometimes slowly, but change is a constant. The old ways become no less effective, however, they still function to the same ends as they did before, it is just that the new techniques allow for maintenance of more "delicate" organisms and more complex webs of marine life. There is now much more for the aquarist to learn: new terminology, new equipment, new techniques, new theory, and lots of new words and ideas.

For example, you may be thinking, "Is *aquaristics* a real word? Why isn't it in the dictionary?" Well, there are a lot of words we use that aren't in the dictionary, yet. Some of them never will get in the dictionary and others just need a definition. So here is my definition of "aquaristics":

Aquaristics is the development and creation of aquariums and/or aquarium systems including the maintenance of aquatic life in aquariums.

In other words, it's what aquarists do, and if it wasn't a real word before, it is now. Both new and old aquaristics are present in this section. And even if you can answer all the questions correctly, we think you'll probably learn something you didn't know before.

1. What is biological filtration?

a) changing ammonia to nitrate

b) changing nitrate to nitrogen gas

c) changing fish waste to ammonia

d) all of the above

2. Why is a "bolt hole" an important feature in combination reef/fish and fish only systems?

a) It allows for attachment of external filter devices.

b) It is an established safe haven where a fish can quickly retreat if it feels threatened.

c) Mechanically inclined fish, such as trigger fish, can practice their construction skills.

d) none of the above

3. If you have a GAC contactor on your system,

a) you have a Great Aquarium Controller unit.

b) you have a Green Algae Cartridge filter.

c) the water is almost always crystal clear.

d) you have a supplementary filter pack on the protein skimmer.

4. Why is it so very important to have tiny weep or spray hole in the input line near the water's surface if your pump input extends down near the bottom of the aquarium?

a) so you can always tell that the pump is working

b) to break up the surface tension of the water surface

c) to prevent a back siphon if the pump dies

d) to keep the aquarium from overflowing

1. d) Biological filtration is the use of the metabolic processes of living organisms to remove toxic waste from the water. Various species of bacteria perform this task and sometimes algae are also used as biological filters. Heterotrophic bacteria break down particulate waste and change it into ammonia (mineralization), nitrifying bacteria change toxic ammonia into non toxic nitrate (oxidization), and denitrifying bacteria change nitrate into nitrogen gas (denitrification). Each of these is a form of biological filtration.

2. b) Most reef fish have a territory that they know very well and this includes caves and protected areas where they can "bolt" or retreat when danger threatens. It is important to take this under consideration when planning the aquascape for a marine aquarium system.

3. c) GAC is the acronym for Granulated Activated Carbon. A contactor is a filter element that enhances water contact with the filter media. Thus a GAC contactor ensures good activated carbon filtration which produces very clear water with no build up of the humic acids that color aquarium water yellow.

4. c) If you pipe water directly from the pump to a point deep within the aquarium, and the pump stops, then you have a pipe full of water between the tank above and the sump below. This creates a siphon, and without a small hole that allows air in to break the siphon, the contents of the aquarium will flow down the input pipe and probably overflow the sump. An aquarist usually only makes this mistake one time.

5. **These are the products of the process of nitrification in the order of their appearance.**

   a) ammonia, nitrite, nitrate
   b) mineralization, nitrification, denitrification
   c) nitrate, nitrite, nitrogen
   d) nitrite, nitrogen, ammonia

6. **It is important to keep the water above the bottom substrate in a marine aquarium at or close to the saturation point of oxygen. What is the saturation level of oxygen in a tropical marine aquarim with a salinity of about 35 ppt (1.026 sg.)?**

   a) 3 ppm
   b) 20 percent
   c) 5 ppt
   d) 7 ppm

7. **What is the ideal salinity for a marine aquarium?**

   a) 32 ppt (1.0237 sg)
   b) 37 ppt (1.0275 sg)
   c) 35 ppt (1.0260 sg)
   d) 30 ppt (1.0222 sg)

8. **A trickle filter should always be used when there is live rock in the aquarium.**

   a) True, ammonia generated by live rock must be removed.
   b) False, water trickles through live rock so it is already a trickle filter.
   c) True, live rock does not have enough surface area.
   d) False, live rock is an efficient biological filter and in most situations, provides adequate biological filtration.

5. a) Nitrification takes over after mineralization and transforms toxic ammonia and nitrite to relatively nontoxic nitrate. Nitrification occurs in nature wherever there is substrate, oxygen, and life.

6. d) Oxygen, the fuel of life, is present in the atmosphere at about 20 percent. It dissolves in seawater until the saturation point is reached. Temperature, salinity and pressure determine the saturation point, which is around 6 to 7 ppm (parts per million) under most marine aquarium conditions.

7. c) On the surface, this is a simple question with a simple answer. 35 ppt is the average salinity of the oceanic environment and one can't go wrong keeping a marine aquarium at this point. In my opinion, however, a slightly lower salinity, about 32 ppt (1.0237sg), provides a little better oxygen content (although not much), makes the fish do a little less metabolic work, and most important, provides a few ppt buffer zone for salinity increase due to evaporation. In other words, if one can't keep a tank at precisely 34 to 35 ppt, then a range of 32 to 35 ppt is better than 35 to 39 ppt. Again, this is a matter of opinion.

8. d) A trickle filter with a high surface area media provides excellent biological filtration for high bioload, fish only systems or densely stocked soft coral reef tanks. It also produces a lot of nitrate, which (along with high phosphate levels) will stimulate strong algal growth, thus a trickle filter is not recommended for stony coral tanks. Live rock does not generate ammonia (unless it has a lot of decaying organic matter) and usually has extensive surface area.

9. If you add carbon dioxide to seawater the pH

a) quickly rises.

b) quickly drops.

c) usually stays the same and then rises.

d) usually stays the same and then drops.

10. In a marine aquarium, nitrification is performed by *Nitrosomonas* bacteria oxidizing ammonia to nitrate and *Nitrobacter* bacteria oxidizing nitrite to nitrate.

a) True, this is the nitrification process as presented in most books and it is correct.

b) False, recent research has shown that *Nitrobacter* is not present in marine biological filters.

c) True, *Nitrosomonas* and *Nitrobacter* are responsible for both terrestrial and aquatic nitrification.

d) False, hetrotrophic bacteria are responsible for nitrification.

11. Why is a drip loop of great importance to marine aquarists?

a) It can prevent electrocution.

b) It slowly delivers *kalkwasser* or other additives to the system.

c) It keeps small fish in an aquarium.

d) It reduces external spray and splash.

12. What is the best size heater for a 100 gallon tank?

a) 400 watts

b) 100 watts

c) 200 watts

d) 500 watts

9. d) When CO_2 is added to seawater it reacts with hydrogen and forms carbonic acid, which could cause the pH to drop. Carbonic acid, however, then immediately forms carbonate and bicarbonate, which in turn join with calcium and form calcium carbonate. This "uses up" the carbonic acid and the pH remains stable. This reaction can move both ways, depending on availability of CO_2 and calcium, and this maintains seawater pH at about 8.2 . This is the seawater buffer system. If more CO_2 is added, and additional calcium is not available, then carbonic acid increases and pH drops, thus at first the pH stays the same and then if excess CO_2 accumulates, or if calcium is depleted, it then drops.

10. b) Recent research by Dr. Tim Hovanec (Marineland Aquarium Products and UCSB) with molecular probes has shown that *Nitrobacter* is not present in marine biological filters. *Nitrosomonas* is present in marine filters but not in freshwater. Nitrification occurs, but it is probably *Nitrospira* that oxidizes nitrite and not *Nitrobacter*. Scientific truth is always subject to change.

11. a) A drip loop is a short downward loop on an electrical cord just before it is plugged into a wall receptacle. This loop ensures that if water collects on the cord, it will drip off rather than seep into the electrical outlet. A small, but very important, safety precaution.

12. c) Under typical conditions, 2 watts per gallon is about right. If the system is in a very cool room then an increase to 300 or 400 watts may be called for.

13. **Of the four possibilities below, what is the best order for passing water from the tank through these four filter elements?**

   a) protein skimmer, biofilter, carbon, particulate filter
   b) particulate filter, biofilter, protein skimmer, carbon
   c) biofilter, particulate filter, carbon, protein skimmer
   d) protein skimmer, particulate filter, biofilter, carbon

14. **If you have a venturi, then you also probably have**

   a) an Italian grandmother.
   b) a protein skimmer.
   c) a trickle filter.
   d) a ventilated light hood.

15. **A constant toxic problem in marine aquaristics is the accumulation of ammonia.**

   a) False, ammonia is quickly transformed to non toxic nitrate.
   b) True, all fish produce ammonia as metabolic waste.
   c) False, an aquarist cannot test for free ammonia.
   d) True, there are no other types of natural toxins in marine aquariums.

16. **Dueling powerheads are useful when**

   a) you need to empty a tank rapidly.
   b) a reef tank needs turbulence.
   c) you need comic relief at a club meeting.
   d) you need to move water around the sump.

13. d) Sure, this is a matter of opinion, but I have reasons for this particular order. Protein skimming removes both particles and dissolved organics before they have a chance to break down, so putting the skimmer first takes maximum advantage of what it can do. A particulate filter could be first, but will not be fully effective unless cleaned daily. A biofilter creates nutrients and makes less nitrate if it is placed after the skimmer and particulate filter. Carbon is most useful in removing color. Putting it last reduces organic fouling.

14. b) In many protein skimmers, a venturi valve injects air into the water flow that enters the skimmers and mixes the air and water into a froth of tiny bubbles. Some powerhead pumps also have a venturi that draws air into the flow as it enters the aquarium.

15. a) Toxic levels of ammonia can only occur in new aquariums where nitrifying bacteria have not yet been established or in aquariums where nitrifying bacteria have been destroyed by antibiotics, dessication, lack of oxygen, or other trauma to the biological filter, thus ammonia toxicity is not a "constant" problem. Under typical circumstances, ammonia is oxidized very quickly into nitrate and never becomes toxic. A far more insidious problem is production of a water borne bacterial toxin that can kill fish in a tank within a few hours.

16. b) Turbulence is the rather random movement of water within the tank. Corals do well when the water is not constantly flowing in the same direction, and setting up powerhead pumps so that the flows interact, helps create beneficial turbulence.

17. If you peek into the fish room and see an aquarist in the act of titrating,

a) quick, run away and close the door behind you.

b) a filter is getting cleaned.

c) a water test is underway.

d) a tank is being filtered.

18. Which of the following set of acronyms/symbols pertain to the same basic function in a marine aquarium system?

a) CO_2, DOC, GMP

b) GAC, NO_3, GPH

c) LPH, CRI, K

d) PAR, VHO, MH

19. What happens if a canister filter is not cleaned regularly?

a) Oxygen is generated.

b) Bacteria populations develop and it becomes a biological filter.

c) The old cans accumulate.

d) The water flow through the filter increases.

20. What is a "bioball"?

a) a plastic structure that provides water space in a trickle filter

b) a plastic ornament for fantasy seascapes

c) an open plastic structure that provides substrate for a biological filter

d) a small ball of detritus, sort of a "marine dust bunny"

17. c) Titration is the process of slowly dripping one solution into another, noting the point of a change in color or other significant transformation, and measuring the amount of solution it took to achieve this change. It is a common procedure used to measure the amount of a chemical in solution and is commonly used in many aquarium water test kits.

18. d) As in most technical endeavors, the marine aquarium hobby has an ample share of acronyms, abbreviations, and symbols. All of d) pertain to lighting. PAR, Photosynthetically Active Radiation (identifies the part of the spectrum that is useful to plants); VHO, Very High Output (identifies high wattage fluorescent lights); and MH, Metal Halide lighting.

19. b) A canister filter is primarily a mechanical filter usually used to remove particulate matter, although if activated carbon is used, then it is a chemical filter. The particulate filter cartridge can be fine and remove tiny particles, or coarse and remove larger particles. It must be cleaned regularly because flow rates through the filter decrease as the pores of the filter clog with debris.

20. c) There are many types and shapes of open plastic structures that provide substrate in trickle filters and those with spherical shape are termed "bioballs". Their main purpose is biological filtration, but they also provide open space to enhance aeration, which is also an important function.

21. **Seawater has a buffer system. What does this mean?**

    a) It does not splash as much as freshwater.
    b) Calcium and iron are balanced.
    c) Algae can use all the CO_2 available.
    d) The pH tends to remain at about 8.2.

22. **If you have a disease problem in an aquarium, the first thing to do is to give it a good shot of an antibiotic.**

    a) True, the first line of defense is an antibiotic, just like when you have a cold.
    b) False, first take out the charcoal filter, then treat.
    c) True, but only after you have first checked for protozoan parasites.
    d) False, antibiotics should be used with great care and only when a bacterial disease is properly diagnosed.

23. **Where is chloramine often found?**

    a) fish foods
    b) tap water
    c) kalkwasser
    d) trace element preparations

24. **One of the following set of three acronyms pertains to one essential chemical element and its activity in all marine aquariums.**

    a) BOD, COD, DO
    b) POP, dKH, UV
    c) DOC, GAC, VHO
    c) DNA, PAR, ORP

21. d) Carbonate, bicarbonate, borate and hydroxide determine the alkalinity of seawater, and in complex reactions with dissolved carbon dioxide and calcium, this determines the pH of seawater. When levels of carbon dioxide and calcium are stable, this buffer system maintains seawater pH at about 8.2.

22. d) Misuse of antibiotics is one of the great tragedies of our age. Treatment of a functioning aquarium system with an antibiotic usually destroys or inhibits the biological filter, does nothing to stem the effects of viral or protozoan disease, and seldom cures the intended target. There is also the danger that it may stimulate the development of antibiotic resistant bacteria, now a major problem. The first step in treating a disease problem is accurate diagnosis of the problem. If antibiotic treatment is required, it should be done in a separate treatment tank.

23. b) Many water treatment plants are using ammonia with chlorine, which forms chloramine, for water treatment. This eliminates formation of trihalomethane, a carcinogen. Free chlorine dissipates rapidly from water, but chloramine is persistent and requires at least double the normal dose of dechlorinator to eliminate chlorine.

24. a) More alphabet soup. It's an easy one, however. Only a) contains three references to oxygen. The O in all three acronyms is a tip off. BOD is Biological Oxygen Demand (oxygen required by living organisms), COD is Chemical Oxygen Demand (oxygen required by chemical processes), and DO is simply Dissolved Oxygen.

25. Does a marine aquarium require a "run in" period of three to four weeks before most fish and invertebrates can survive?

a) Yes, because sensitive fish can die of ammonia poisoning in a newly set up marine system.

b) No, with live rock and live sand, biological filtration is established at inception of the system.

c) Both a) and b) are correct.

d) Both a) and b) are incorrect.

26. If you have too much detritus, your aquarium

a) smells bad.

b) has an algae problem.

c) is dirty and needs to be cleaned.

d) has excess phosphate.

27. What is the most important reason for good water movement within and around a reef tank?

a) so that the nutrients that corals need are spread evenly around the tank

b) to prevent development of oxygen poor water layers

c) good water movement prevents formation of an "envelope" of stagnant water around living corals

d) to wash away the stinging cells of corals before they can affect other animals.

28. Corals need PAR (microEinsteins per square meter per second) in amounts of

a) Huh? that's a lot of teeny tiny Einsteins. I didn't know that they had cloned him.

b) 30 to 1800

c) 5000 to 20000

d) 10 to 500

25. c) Now how can a) and b) both be correct if they are apparently in direct opposition to each other? Well bacterial colonies that provide biological filtration take weeks to establish in a marine system set up without live rock, while properly conditioned live rock used in a reef or fish system provides "instant" biological filtration. Be aware, however, that even with ample amounts of live rock and live sand, new reef tanks still go through various developmental cycles.

26. c) Detritus is the organic particulate matter that accumulates in filters and on tank bottoms. Low phosphate levels are important in reef tanks, and since phosphate is present in detritus, it is usually necessary to remove detritus from reef tanks. Detritus will make the aquarium smell bad only if the water is removed or if there is little or no oxygen in the water.

27. c) Some corals require strong water movement and some do well with weak flows, but without good water movement (preferably water flows variable in strength and direction), respiration, feeding, and tissue growth are compromised, the coral suffers, and the potential for disease is enhanced.

28. b) PAR is the acronym for Photosynthetically Active Radiation, which is measured in microEinsteins per square meter per second ($\mu E/m^2/s$). This is the part of the spectrum most useful to plants. Dana Riddle reports that corals need PAR in the range of 30 to 1780 $\mu E/m^2/s$. Various bulbs produce various amounts of PAR. To find the approximate PAR produced by a 10000 K ML bulb, divide the lux at any point in the tank by 30.

29. What is a protein skimmer?

    a) a foam fractionator

    b) a chemical filter

    c) a mechanical filter

    d) all of the above

30. Most aquarium heaters are constructed with an electrical resistance coil in a water tight, glass bulb. What should an aquarist always remember to do with a heater?

    a) Never unplug the heater before lowering the water level in the tank.

    b) Leave the thermostat set at the lowest point.

    c) Check the heater frequently to make sure it is working properly.

    d) Never leave it loaded.

31. What is the best color temperature range of the light bulbs above a reef tank?

    a) 5500 to 6000 °K.

    b) 6500 to 15000 °K.

    c) 10000 to 15000 °K.

    d) all of the above

32. Which group of three terms defines the complete process of biological filtration?

    a) ammonia, nitrite, nitrate

    b) mineralization, nitrification, denitrification

    c) nitrate, nitrite, nitrogen

    d) nitrite, nitrogen, ammonia

29. d) Another name, in fact the original term, for a protein skimmer is "foam fractionator". Long before "protein skimmers" were used by aquarists, they were in use for separation of various surface active compounds from aqueous solutions. Skimmers are chemical filters in that they remove dissolved compounds and mechanical filters in that they also remove tiny particulates from marine aquarium water.

30. c) A good aquarist **always unplugs** the heater before lowing the water level. The glass bulb around the heating coils will overheat and crack or shatter if the heater is not immersed in water when it is on. Also, check tank temperatures frequently. Heater thermostats can easily stick in the on or off position and turn the tank into a hot tub or ice bath, both very bad for fish.

31. b) Corals need light in the blue range of the spectrum to provide energy for photosynthesis by *zooxanthellae*. Yet we see best with light at a color temperature closer to sunlight, 5500 °K. Providing light in a range of 6500 to 10000 °K or even up to 15000 °K gives a good blue component and still provides the white/yellow light that is more normal for human eyes.

32. b) Biological filtration is the activity of living organisms on particulate and metabolic waste that eliminates or reduces toxic substances and/or nutrients. It includes changing organic wastes into non organic nutrients (mineralization), changing toxic ammonia and nitrite into nitrate (nitrification) and changing nitrate into nitrogen gas (denitrification). a) c) and d) are just products of this process.

33. In which of the following groups do all three things perform the one basic, absolutely essential, life support function for captive aquatic life, despite any differences in their basic purpose?

a) ion exchange resin, live sand, activated carbon

b) undergravel filter, protein skimmer, live rock

c) tiny castle, activated carbon, algae filter

d) protein skimmer, trickle filter, air lift

34. Big problems can develop when the following gas is supersaturated in a marine aquarium system.

a) nitrogen

b) oxygen

c) carbon dioxide

d) all of the above

35. What is the approximate amount of dissolved calcium in natural seawater?

a) 200 ppm

b) 400 ppm

c) 450 ppt

d) 500 ppm

36. $2NO_3^- + 12H^+ \rightarrow N_2 + 6H_2O$ is the equation for

a) nitrification.

b) denitrification.

c) mineralization.

d) photosynthesis.

33. d) The most essential function for life in an aquarium, before even biological filtration, is gas exchange (aeration). This is the import of oxygen and the export of carbon dioxide. Without gas exchange, desirable life cannot exist within the aquarium. Of the above three groups, although all the devices function to improve life in the aquarium (except, perhaps, for the tiny castle), only in **d)** do all devices directly enhance one function, gas exchange.

34. a) In water, nitrogen is usually always at equilibrium with atmospheric pressure. However, if nitrogen is forced into water under pressure, as may happen if air and water are mixed in the intake line of a powerful pump, then the nitrogen dissolved under pressure will bubble out of the water in the form of very tiny bubbles. It will also bubble out of the tissues of aquatic animals and cause the "bends".

35. b) The range of calcium in natural seawater is about 380 to 450 ppm. Calcium levels are rather stable in the oceanic waters that wash over coral reefs, so it is always available to the plants and animals that form these reefs. (ppm, parts per million; ppt, parts per thousand.)

36. b) OK, so you have to know a little chemistry, but really all the chemistry you have to know to get the right answer is that N is the symbol for nitrogen, H is the symbol for hydrogen, H_2O is water, and NO_3 is nitrate. If you know this, and you should, then you know that you are starting with nitrate, breaking it apart, and ending up with nitrogen gas and water, which is denitrification.

37. Which group has three of the most common and dangerous of marine fish protozoan parasites?

a) *Cryptocaryon*, black ick, lymphocystis

b) *Amyloodinium, Cryptocaryon, Brooklynella*

c) *Amyloodinium, Brooklynella, Vibrio*

d) *Mycobacterium, Cryptocaryon*, fin rot

38. The Kelvin scale is

a) a measure of temperature.

b) a measure of light.

c) a type of fish scale.

d) a measure of weight.

39. When do marine aquarists use reverse osmosis?

a) when processing aquarium water through a membrane to remove various nutrient salts and other pollutants

b) to move a full tank away from the wall

c) to produce fresh water from seawater

d) to process tap water to remove various nutrient salts and other pollutants before aquarium use

40. The Archimedes screw pump is

a) found in high end protein skimmers.

b) what an unwary aquarist might get at a discount.

c) a lift pump that does not damage plankton.

d) a circular air lift device.

37. b) There are many forms of disease and distress that can afflict marine fish. It is all important to correctly identify the cause of disease or distress before treatment. *Vibrio, Mycobacterium,* and fin rot are bacterial; lymphocystis is viral; and black ich is a flatworm. Only b) are all protozoan parasites.

38. a) There are three temperature scales: Fahrenheit, Celsius (aka Centigrade), and Kelvin. Kelvin units are the same as Celsius, but the Kelvin scale begins at absolute zero (-273 ° C). The color of light is defined by the temperature of the source and so light bulbs are rated by the color temperature of the light they emit. Low temperatures (2000 to 3000 °K) emit red light and high temperatures (7000 to 20000 °K) emit more blue light. Natural sunlight is about 5500 °K.

39. d) Reverse osmosis is a water purification process that pushes water through a membrane fine enough to remove dissolved molecules. Marine aquarists produce RO water from tapwater to make up artificial seawater and to replace evaporated water. This reduces the accumulation of phosphate and other nutrients in reef tanks.

40. c) The Archimedes screw pump consists of a long tube with a course flanged, screw type shaft that extends down through the tube, and as it rotates, lifts water up the tube to a higher level. Long used in sewerage and agriculture, such pumps may have application where damage to microorganisms by conventional pumps must be avoided.

41. A biowheel is a very efficient biological filter because

a) it continuously aerates the filter substrate and provides optimum conditions for growth of nitrifying bacteria.

b) it provides a recreational experience for nitrifying bacteria.

c) it efficiently aerates aquarium water.

d) these rotating biological contactors concentrate the nutrients on the biological substrate.

42. Why is it not a good idea to use transparent tubes and pipes in an aquarium system?

a) Water flows more efficiently through opaque pipes.

b) Privacy, all kinds of little critters live in those pipes and they need their privacy.

c) PVC glue works better on white or gray pipes.

d) Algae does not grow where there is no light, so opaque pipes do not foul with algal growths.

43. A marine aquarium kept at 27 degrees Celsius is also at what point on the Fahrenheit scale?

a) 60 degrees F

b) 75 degrees F

c) 80 degrees F

d) 77 degrees F

44. Elemental copper is highly toxic. Why would anyone put copper in a marine aquarium?

a) to enhance the immune system of marine fish

b) to reduce the aggressive tendencies of trigger fish

c) to kill the dinospore stage of *Amyloodinium*

d) to kill *Cryptocaryon* and bacteria

41. a) Optimum growth of nitrifying bacteria colonies requires ample substrate with low site competition from other bacteria and a good supply of oxygenated water. Rotating biological contactors (biowheels) have provided biological filtration for aquaculture and sewage plants for many years. Just aeration without substrate does not provide biolgical filtration However, the concomitant aeration of aquarium water by biowheel filters is a bonus.

42. d) Well, duh. Over time, algae growth can clog or severely restrict water flow through a transparent pipe or tube. Water may flow more efficiently through opaque pipes but only if the transparent pipes have internal algal growth, a function of the algae, not the pipe.

43. c) This is one conversion in the tropical aquarium range that is accurate at whole numbers on both F and C scales. It is useful to remember that 27 degrees Celsius is exactly equal to 80 degrees F.

44. c) Copper, complexed with citric acid, at a dosage of 0.15 to 0.2 ppm in a quarantine or treatment tank is a very effective treatment for *Amyloodinium ocellatum,* also called ich, marine velvet, and coral fish disease. This parasitic dinoflagellate affects marine fish and looks like an almost dusty white coating on the fins and body. Of all the parasitic fish diseases, this is the most common and most deadly to almost all fish. Copper treatment does not greatly affect bacteria (it may enhance *Vibrio* growth) and may negatively affect the immune system of fish. It will also kill most corals.

45. A low pH in a marine aquarium, 7.5 to 7.9 can indicate

a) accumulation of carbon dioxide.

b) accumulation of nitrate.

c) loss of alkalinity.

d) all of the above

46. The same volume of all brands of artificial sea salts will make up to the same salinity when dissolved into the same volume of water.

a) True, salt is salt.

b) False, some salts may have more water in them than others.

c) True, the same number of ions is released from the same volume of salt.

d) False, small salt grains have more salt in them than large grained salt and this must be taken into account.

47. We can estimate salinity with a hydrometer because of

a) water pressure.

b) Archimedes' principle.

c) Pascal's law.

d) atmospheric pressure.

48. What is the most important type of filtration for a fish only marine aquarium system?

a) biological filtration

b) protein skimming

c) UV sterilization

d) activated carbon filtration

45. d) pH is a useful indicator of a variety of problems. Low pH can indicate the need for a water change, the need for increased aeration, the need for alkalinity replacement and a number of other problems as well.

46. b) There is, or there can be, significant differences in the amount of actual salt in various brands of salt mixes. Hydrated salts (salts with water within the salt structure) cost less and dissolve more quickly, but contain less actual salt than anhydrous (water free) salts. This can cause a difference of up to 12% between the actual salinity that results from the same volume of different salt mixes. For accuracy, use the recommended measure of each particular brand of salt and not just a standard volume measure.

47. b) Eureka! Which is what Archimedes hollered in the bathtub when he realized that a body immersed in a fluid is buoyed up by a force equal to the weight of the displaced fluid. A hydrometer float is pushed upward by a force equal to the weight of the volume of water it displaces, and since salt water weighs more than fresh water, the float floats higher in salt water. A calibrated scale provides the specific gravity reading. The concept of specific gravity is based on Archimedes' principle.

48. a) Fish and uneaten fish food produce a lot of organic waste. This must be handled by biological filtration, thus the first requirement for a fish tank is a good biological filter. Other types of filtration are helpful, especially protein skimming, but biological filtration is the filtration foundation of a fish tank.

49. What is the main function of a trickle filter?

a) to kill bacteria

b) to perform biological filtration

c) to aerate aquarium water

d) to remove trickles from the aquarium

50. What is the best use of activated carbon in an aquarium?

a) removal of ammonia

b) removal of carbon monoxide

c) adding oxygen to old water

d) removal of coloring dyes from the water

51. Why is the following formula L x W x H divided by 231 = X so very useful to aquarists?

a) It gives you the number of gallons that must be exchanged in a tank to refresh the water.

b) When inch measurements are used, it provides the number of gallons in a square or rectangular tank.

c) It gives you the weight of the tank filled with water.

d) The length, weight and height of the aquarist is input to provide the proper height of the aquarium stand.

52. Ozone is sometimes used in marine aquarium systems. Addition of this form of oxygen

a) has to be done within a reactor to prevent ozone from entering the aquarium.

b) boosts the redox potential of the water.

c) oxidizes dissolved organic compounds.

d) all of the above

49. b) Although this is apparently a straightforward question with a simple answer, it could be a little tricky. Biological filtration is the basic function of a trickle filter, and a trickle filter is a very good biofilter because air and water are actively mixed throughout the filter giving the nitrifying bacteria all the oxygen they need. A trickle filter is also an aeration device. But basically, a trickle filter is a biological filter and aeration is a bonus.

50. d) Activated carbon, usually called Granular Activated Carbon (GAC), is a substance that contains billions of micropores that are so small that they trap molecules of various sizes, thus removing them from liquid or gas environments. Although a wide variety of organic and inorganic molecules are collected by activated carbon, the most useful application of GAC is to remove the yellow organic dyes that discolor aquarium waters.

51. b) Surely you didn't miss this one. This is one of the most useful formulas in all aquaridom. It is used to calculate the gallons needed to completely or partly fill a tank. Also very useful in calculating tank volumes for medications in a quarantine tank.

52. d) Ozone can be a useful tool for the aquarist, but it can also create problems if it is not applied with care and knowledge. It is a very strong oxidizer and can damage equipment and kill fish and invertebrates if allowed to remain in the water after treatment. Most aquarists are better off upgrading with a protein skimmer instead of using ozone.

53. A marine aquarium system with an meq/L of 2.5 has

a) a low calcium level.

b) a salinity problem.

c) a good alkalinity level.

d) a need for *kalkwasser*.

54. The salinity of the water in a typical marine aquarium should be kept between about 1.023 and 1.026

a) False, because 1.023 and 1.026 are a measure of specific gravity, not salinity.

b) True, because this is at and just below the range of natural sea water.

c) False, because it should be 023 and 026.

d) True, because salinity and specific gravity are the same thing.

55. Why is photoperiod important to aquarists?

a) Keeping the lights on at night makes for better observation of the tank.

b) This brackets the best time to take photographs of the tank.

c) One can nap at conferences during the slide shows.

d) The period of exposure to light for marine animals should be within the normal range.

56. The most important type of filter to put on a marine reef tank is

a) a biological filter.

b) a protein skimmer.

c) UV sterilization unit.

d) an activated carbon filter.

53. c) Alkalinity is measured in MillEQuivalents per Liter (Meq/L), and natural seawater is about 2.1 to 2.5. A meq/L of 2.5 shows that the aquarium water has an acceptable amount of carbonate/bicarbonate and that the seawater buffer system is in good shape.

54. a) Salinity and specific gravity are very different. Salinity is a measure of the salts in seawater and is measured in parts per thousand salt (o/oo) while specific gravity of seawater is the ratio of the weight of a given volume of seawater to the weight of the same volume of pure freshwater. *Approximate* salinity can be determined from specific gravity and since this is a relatively easy way to obtain an estimate of salinity, it is widely used by aquarists. (Note: the zero before 023 and 026 is meaningless unless there is a decimal point before the 0.)

55. d) Photoperiod is the length of daylight. It varies seasonally in all areas of the world except the equator, where day and night are equal. It is not good for a marine aquarium to be under constant light or to have too few hours of light per day. Most tropical marine organisms do well on 12 to 14 hours of light per 24 hour day.

56. b) A typical reef tank holds mostly invertebrates with relatively few fish. These reef tanks usually contain a lot of live rock and live sand and maintain low levels of algal nutrients. Live rock and live sand easily take care of the requirement for biological filtration and this then puts the need for effective protein skimming, which exports dissolved nutrients, at the top of the list.

57. If the pump on an aquarium system for a 125 gallon aquarium produces 45 gph (0.75 gpm, 170 lph) at the input to the tank, then what is the number of tank volume turnovers in 24 hours?

   a) None, this is a trick question.

   b) 10

   c) 8.6

   d) 6.5

58. What is "algal turf scrubbing"?

   a) using an abrasive pad to clean algae off the tank sides

   b) balancing nutrient input in a marine aquarium system with regularly harvested algae growth

   c) use of "high technology" in aquarium management

   d) cleaning detritus from growths of macro algae

59. The element calcium, so important to the health of reef tanks, is a type of

   a) stone

   b) metal

   c) chalk

   d) silicon

60. What type of filter is a fluidized bed?

   a) chemical filter

   b) mechanical filter

   c) biological filter

   d) all of the above

57. c) Just do the math. 45 gph x 24 hours = 1080, which divided by 125 gallons = 8.64. It could have been a trick question. If it had asked for the number of system turnovers, then you couldn't answer it because the volume of the sump and external filters was not given.

58. b) "Natural systems", systems that balance the nutrients produced by animal waste with nutrient uptake and transformation by bacteria and plants have been around since the mid 1800's. In the last decade this concept has been reborn with greater knowledge of the process and applications specific to marine systems. Algal turf scrubbing has been popularized mainly by Dr. Walter Addy of the Smithsonian Institution. "Turf" refers to the firm algal base that remains on the scrubber plate.

59. b) Yep, calcium is a silvery metallic element with an atomic number of 20 and an atomic weight of 40.08. As calcium carbonate, it does make up limestone and chalk, and it is the building material for bone and coral skeletons, but the element calcium is metallic in chemical structure.

60. c) Fluidized bed filters have been used in sewage treatment plants and high intensity aquaculture for many years. They have relatively recently been adapted for aquarium use. Water travels slowly upward through a column of sand, keeping the sand grains suspended in the water column, thus preventing accretion and compaction. They are very efficient biological filters and are best suited to high bioload situations.

61. Mechanical filtration is

 a) a machine that filters aquarium water.

 b) an automatic filter.

 c) the removal of particles from aquarium water.

 d) all of the above.

62. How can you tell if a protein skimmer is working properly?

 a) It is filled with tiny white bubbles.

 b) It makes a whizzing noise.

 c) It produces so much foam that it must be emptied very often.

 d) It typically produces several ounces of dark foamate every day or two.

63. The alkalinity of seawater is

 a) the capacity of the water to resist drops in pH.

 b) the capacity of the water to maintain calcium levels.

 c) the ratio of calcium to carbon dioxide.

 d) a result of treatment with too many fizzy tablets.

64. Carbon dioxide is generated by all living things in the aquarium (It is used by plants during photosynthetic activity, but is also released by plants during darkness). What happens when excess carbon dioxide is accumulated in aquarium water?

 a) Tiny bubbles develop in the water.

 b) pH of the water can drop to dangerous levels.

 c) The growth of algae is severely stunted.

 d) Fish are stronger and healthier.

61. c) There are two types of pollutants in aquarium water: dissolved compounds and free floating particles. The particles may be very tiny, or even large enough to see without magnification. A mechanical filter physically traps and holds particles until they dissolve or are removed by filter cleaning.

62. d) A protein skimmer has to be adjusted for each system. It is not working properly if it produces too much or too little foamate (the dark liquid produced when the foam disintegrates). The true test of proper operation is not the presence of many bubbles (although many tiny bubbles are necessary), but the relatively constant production of a dark foamate. Note that low bioload systems produce relatively little foamate while high bioload systems usually produce large amounts of foamate.

63. a) Alkalinity does not refer to a specific element or compound. It is the capacity of the water to neutralize acid. In seawater, alkalinity is created by the presence of carbonates, bicarbonates, borates, and hydroxides (all anions) that function to chemically bind a certain amount of acids (cations) and this prevents a drop in pH. The higher the alkalinity of the water (the more available carbonate and bicarbonate), the more acid can be accepted without a pH drop.

64. b) It is just as important to vent excess carbon dioxide from the water of a marine aquarium as it is to bring in oxygen. Both are accomplished by good aeration. Excess carbon dioxide lowers the pH and may cause serious metabolic problems for fish.

65. An addition or change of carbon which causes a rapid reduction in the amount of humic acids (yellow coloring, *gelbstoff*) in a reef tank is always a good thing.

a) False, it may remove some trace elements and it may also stress and even bleach corals.

c) True, yellow water is unsightly in reef tanks.

d) False, it has been recently shown that GAC traps *zooxanthellae* preventing recapture by corals.

c) True, because it removes any regurgitated methane gas that might be generated by deep sediments.

66. Why is a freshwater bath often helpful to marine fish.

a) It stimulates the immune system.

b) It flushes away excess mucus.

c) It removes many external parasites.

d) all of the above

67. A plenum, an open area of dead water space under a layer of coral sand at the bottom of a reef tank, provides

a) the anaerobic conditions that allow denitrification.

b) the space required by nitrifying bacteria.

c) diffusion of carbon dioxide.

d) for reproduction of live sand organisms.

68. Which group of three processes all perform the same basic function?

a) ozonation, UV sterilization, particulate filtration

b) protein skimming, activated carbon, ozonation

c) heating, cooling, lighting

d) water movement, trickle filtration, ion exchange resin

65. a) Granulated activated carbon (GAC) is used in aquarium systems to remove or reduce humic acids that color the water yellow. In reef systems, rapid reduction in water color may increase the UV radiation that reaches corals and cause a bleaching response. Also, humic acids may make certain trace elements (iron) available to *zooxanthellae* and rapid removal may negatively impact corals.

66. c) Placing a marine fish in freshwater, of the same temperature and pH as the saltwater, for 1 to 5 minutes has the effect of rapidly changing the osmotic pressure of the water around the fish. Small external parasites on skin, fins, and gills cannot withstand this abrupt change and either die or drop off the fish. This procedure is useful when parasites are observed or as a precaution measure for hardy fish before quarantine.

67. a) A plenum is part of the marine aquarium system developed by Dr. Jean Jaubert of the Monaco Aquarium. Whether it is more effective than just a deep coral sand layer is still controversial, but it supposedly maintains the anaerobic conditions (a sequestered water layer low in oxygen) necessary for denitrification, which also helps to dissolve aragonite (a form of calcium carbonate) in coral sand and maintain alkalinity and calcium levels.

68. b) All three of these processes perform Chemical Filtration. Protein skimming attracts dissolved molecules to air bubbles and then removes them, activated carbon traps dissolved organic molecules, and ozonation destroys organic molecules through oxidation.

69. What makes a siphon work?

a) magic, just pure magic

b) gravity

c) inertia

d) atmospheric pressure

70. What is a calcium reactor?

a) He keels over in a dead faint when the test shows a level of only 100 ppm calcium.

b) It is a device that responds to low calcium by increasing the drip rate of *kalkwasser*.

c) a device that mixes "coral sand" ($CaCO_3$) with CO_2 within a container to produce dissolved calcium carbonate

d) a device with a probe that senses the level of dissolved calcium

71. What are the products of the process of denitrification in the order of their appearance?

a) ammonia, nitrite, nitrate

b) mineralization, nitrification, denitrification

c) nitrate, nitrite, nitrogen

d) nitrite, nitrogen, ammonia

72. What is the best way to remove red slime algae from a reef tank?

a) The only way is physical removal, keep siphoning off the algae until it goes away.

b) Use the antibiotic erythromycin at 10 mg per gallon.

c) Employ extensive water changes, 50% each week until the algae dissipates.

d) Eliminate as much phosphate as possible.

69. d) Creating a siphon, moving water from a higher point to a lower point through a closed tube filled with water, is one of the most useful tricks known to aquarists— but why does it work? Water flows downhill in response to gravitational force, but gravity can't make water flow upward. The surface water level of two vessels connected by a tube filled with water will remain equal regardless of how much water is in each vessel or where the ends of the tube are placed within each vessel. Gravity and inertia help out on the downward leg, but they can't make the siphon work. It's differential atmospheric pressure on the open surface of each vessel that makes it work.

70. c) One of the great challenges in operating a reef tank heavily stocked with stony corals and/or coralline algae is to maintain adequate levels of calcium carbonate, balanced with the proper alkalinity. A calcium reactor is an effective way of maintaining proper calcium and alkalinity levels in a reef aquarium.

71. c) Denitrification takes place under anaerobic conditions (very low oxygen, less than about 1 ppm). Complete denitrification transforms nitrate into nitrogen gas and removes this nutrient from the water.

72. d) There are methods that will temporarily remove red slime algae, such as a) and b), but the best and most permanent method is to reduce phosphate in the system water. To do this, raise alkalinity and use *kalkwasser* to precipitate phosphate already in the system and then feed sparingly and use RO water for evaporation make up and water changes to reduce phosphate introduction.

73. What is the "curing" of live rock?

a) the use of antibiotics to remove bacteria

b) drying the rock to develop a hard, organic surface

c) providing for the decay and removal of excess organic material on and in the rock before use

d) stimulating the fermentation of sponges on the rock

74. What is a biological undergravel filter?

a) a filter that is located under the gravel bed

b) the substrate above a perforated plate that rests just above the bottom of an aquarium

c) a filter that cleans the sand at the bottom of the tank

d) all of the above

75. One of the main sources of unwanted phosphate addition to reef tanks is

a) algae growth.

b) make up water from wells and city supplies.

c) detritus accumulations in marine systems.

d) bird droppings.

76. Why is "never fill the sump" very good advice?

a) It's always a good idea to save space in case you need to add water later.

b) Extra salt water in a system just costs more money.

c) More water than you need in the sump just reduces the frequency of water exchange in the main tank.

d) If the sump is full, and the electric goes out and the "working water" in the system drains into the sump, then the sump will overflow.

73. c) Fresh "live rock" contains organic detritus, dead organisms, and some live organisms that can not survive. Curing the rock consists of removal of obvious dead material and then holding the rock in a marine system for some time while heterotrophic bacteria clean up excess dead organic material. The rock can then be placed in an aquarium without an accompanying load of dead organic matter. Fermentation of sponges? Chuckle.

74. b) The so called "undergravel" filter was the first really successful biological filter for a marine aquarium. It is constructed of a layer of sand and/or gravel placed on a raised perforated plate located on the bottom of the tank. Water is forced through the sand/gravel filter by drawing it up to the surface of the tank through tubes that extend down through the filter plate. Extensive colonies of nitrifying bacteria grow on the sand/gravel substrate and transform the ammonia in the water into nitrate as it passes through the substrate. Thus it is the bottom substrate itself that is the biological filter.

75. b) Phosphate is bad news for reef tanks (also fish tanks), and it is most commonly introduced in fresh water that is used to make up for evaporation or used to mix up artificial seawater. Other sources are some types of activated carbon, fish food, and decaying fish or invertebrates. Also, do not allow your parrot to perch above the tank.

76. d) OK, so it's obvious why you shouldn't fill up the sump, but it is something you should think about if you never thought about it before.

77. **Which of the following group of three all perform one very essential function, despite any differences in their basic purpose.**

   a) protein skimmer, plenum, trickle filter
   b) undergravel filter, algae filter, live rock
   c) ion exchange resin, live sand, activated carbon
   d) air lift, activated carbon, algae filter

78. **If a reef aquarist has RTN in his or her tank, then**

   a) the corals are suffering from Rapid Tissue Necrosis.
   b) it has a beautiful specimen of sun coral, Red Tubastraea Nemoricole.
   c) a bigger pump is required to service the Rapid Turnover Need.
   d) none of the above

79. **When is a new marine aquarium system ready for the addition of permanent display organisms?**

   a) when the substrate settles and the water clears
   b) when the initial ammonia level drops to near 0
   c) when the nitrite (NO_2) level drops to near 0
   d) when the nitrate (NO_3) level drops to near 0

80. **Why is phosphate accumulation in reef tanks very bad?**

   a) It is a "crystal poison" and interferes with calcification and growth in corals.
   b) It is a nutrient and fuels the growth of unwanted algae.
   c) It becomes part of the organic compounds that form detritus and is then difficult to remove from the tank.
   d) all of the above

77. b) The function is, of course, Biological Filtration. Nitrifying bacteria are the most useful life forms that perform biological filtration, but algal growth is also useful in removal of ammonia and other nutrients from aquarium water.

78. a) Soon after reef aquarists learned to keep and propagate SPS corals, primarily *Acorpora* sp., Rapid Tissue Necrosis, RTN, reared its ugly head. RTN is apparently caused by various bacteria which cause a rapid disintegration of tissue along the coral branches. It can be controlled by certain antibiotics, but the best recovery method seems to be the cutting and reestablishment of unaffected parts of the colony.

79. c) The "run in cycle" of a marine aquarium system begins with ammonia, moves to nitrite and when all the proper bacterial populations are established, nitrate begins to accumulate. Typically, ammonia builds up for about a week, nitrite accumulations follow and build for two to three weeks and then rapidly decline to nearly zero. The tank is then accumulating nitrate and is ready to accept new organisms. Even a reef tank with an initial load of biologically active live rock (an "instant" biological filter) should be checked for ammonia and nitrite during the first few months.

80. d) Phosphate is an essential element of life and is always present in some form in marine systems. But because it stimulates algal growth and inhibits coral growth, phosphate input into a reef system must be reduced as much as possible to prevent excessive accumulation.

Reef and Sea

A marine aquarium, whether just a fish tank or the complex web of life in a reef tank, is but a reflection of the natural environment: a contained and limited representation of marine aquatic life. Aquarists first worked at keeping marine fish alive and well in captive environments very unlike their natural environment. Fortunately for both fish and aquarists, modern marine aquariums began to incorporate live rock, macro algae, soft and hard corals; and now even the deep sand substrates of natural coral reefs are part and parcel of the newest generation of marine aquaristics. Even though captive duplication of the entire coral reef environment is an impossible dream, aquarists are creating reflections of nature that are getting closer and closer to the natural environment.

Obviously, a knowledge of reef and sea, the natural environment, is essential to the development of modern reef aquariums. The more we know about life on a coral reef, the more successful we will be as marine aquarists. The following questions cover the field. Some are directly pertinent to keeping a marine aquarium and some pertain only to the natural environment. If you get them all right, or even 80%, you're far more knowledgeable of reef and sea than we.

1. **The world's ocean basins are vast and deep reservoirs of water. Tides, winds, storms, and the Coriolis effect move this water around the world. How long does it take for world wide water mixing and exchange to take place in these ocean basins ?**

    a) 10 years

    b) 100 years

    c) 1000 years

    d) 10000 years

2. **Mollusk shells scattered around a small hole at the base of the reef is sure sign that**

    a) a grouper lives there.

    b) a spiny lobster has moved in.

    c) an octopus occupies that hole.

    d) a nest of starfish lies under the reef.

3. **What famous "living fossil" was found still alive in the deep waters off the Comoro Islands in 1938?**

    a) chambered Nautilus

    b) the coelacanth, *Latimeria chalumnae*

    c) the giant isopod

    d) the deep sea, sea lily, *Holopus rangi*

4. **Sea fans, *Gorgonia* sp., those large, flat fan shaped gorgonians, usually grow in a manner that orients them**

    a) with the broad aspect of the fan facing the prevailing currents.

    b) with the fan edgewise to the prevailing currents.

    c) with the fan oriented to catch the most sunlight.

    d) without any particular positioning.

1. c) Oceanographers estimate that it takes 1000 years for the seawater in the worlds ocean basins to mix from basin to basin.

2. c) Most large predators on a coral reef can not handle the hard, almost impenetrable shell of most large mollusks. An exception is the octopus, who with its strong arms, grasping suckers and sharp beak can enter the shell and feed on many mollusks.

3. b) Crossopterygian fishes, the early lobe finned fish that were ancestral to early amphibians, were well known from the fossil record. In December of 1938 a fishing vessel off the shores of South Africa caught such an unusual fish that it was sent to a local museum. This fish, previously unknown to science, turned out to be a coelacanth, a true "living fossil". Since then many more coelacanths have been taken at 230 to 1000 feet, and a few even observed alive for some time. The behavior and anatomy of this fish have provided much information on the evolution of vertebrates.

4. a) When you observe sea fans growing on the reef, you are likely to notice that they are all growing with the same orientation, a response that assures maximum exposure of the polyps in the net-like matrix to the plankton that streams by in the prevailing currents.

5. What are the five major ocean basins?

  a) Pacific, Atlantic, Mediterranean, Indian, Antarctic

  b) Pacific, Atlantic, Arctic, Antarctic, Indian

  c) Pacific, Indian, Atlantic, Caribbean, Arctic

  d) Gulf of Mexico, Mediterranean, Atlantic, Indian, Pacific

6. What is the most obvious difference between hard corals and anemones?

  a) the structure of the tentacles

  b) secretion of a stony skeleton by hard corals

  c) the size, anemones being much larger

  d) corals are colonial and anemones are solitary

7. Two examples of pleuston are

  a) *Halobates* and *Physalia.*

  b) *Dendronephthya* and *Cladiella.*

  c) fish and chips.

  d) a veliger and a nauplius.

8. The fuel for all life on Earth is the energy developed from the process of photosynthesis.

  a) True, plants at the bottom of the food chain produce all life energy through photosynthesis.

  b) False, life based on hydrogen sulphide exists on the ocean bottom.

  c) True, sunlight is required for all life.

  d) False, the "marine snow" that drops into the deep sea is also a basis for life.

5. b) These are the major oceanic basins of the world, not the "seven seas" of ancient lore. They are deep basins separating the continents which project upward and "float" on the liquid mantle of the earth's interior. The Antarctic Ocean is also known as the Southern Ocean.

6. b) Corals and anemones are very much alike in structure of the soft tissues. There are solitary corals as well as colonial anemones (Zoanthiniaria) and great size variations occur in both groups.

7. a) To get this one right (without just a lucky guess) you would have to know that pleuston are those members of the plankton that actually float on the surface of the water, and that *Physalia* are the man o' war jellyfish that have a float that extends above the surface, and that *Halobates* is the only truly oceanic insect, a water strider that walks on the surface tension of the water. You didn't expect to get every one right, did you?

8. b) In 1977, it was discovered that abundant life: tube worms, clams, siphonophores, crabs, and even fish, lived in the utter blackness of the deep sea in areas around hydrothermal vents (black smokers). The energy source for this web of life is chemosynthesis by about 200 varieties of bacteria that feed on the energy rich hydrogen sulfide molecule. Other sources of life energy in the deeps - "marine snow" and the bodies of whales and other large animals - initially derived energy from photosynthesis near the surface of the sea.

9. An "osculum" is a structure found in

   a) starfish.
   b) sponges.
   c) tunicates.
   d) gastropods.

10. What is the process by which corals and coraline algae build reefs?

   a) calcinosis
   b) calcification
   c) calefaction
   d) calceolate

11. Many sharks are ovoviviparous which means

   a) that the young are born fully formed after the yolk sac has been absorbed.
   b) that the young feed on eggs that are released into the uterus.
   c) that the young are released within an egg sac.
   d) Ovo what?

12. Of the groups below, which set of two organisms occupy the lowest trophic level?

   a) tunas and barracuda
   b) diatoms and flagellates
   c) copepods and rotifers
   d) damselfish and whale sharks

9. b) The "osculum" is the central opening(s) at the top of the sponge where water exits after being drawn in through small pores on the side of the sponge.

10. b) An easy one, right? Calcification is the process that corals use to produce insoluble "limestone" from dissolved calcium carbonate. Calcinosis is the abnormal deposition of calcium salts in the body, calefaction is the act of heating, and calceolate is the shape of a shoe. See, I told you you would learn something.

11. a) Compared to the bony fishes, sharks produce very few young. Fertilization is internal and the young develop within a two horned uteri from large yolked eggs. Ovoviviparous reproduction means that the fertilized eggs, maintained within the uterus of the female, gain sustenance from the egg yolk until they are mature enough for birth. They are born fully developed and ready to begin feeding. The low reproductive rate of sharks makes it very easy to overfish the stocks of these top level predators.

12. b) A food web is made up of many trophic levels. At the bottom of the food web, or food chain, are the primary producers, plants that use nutrients and sunlight to produce organic matter. Next are the animals that feed directly on these primary producers, followed by the animals that feed on those in the second level and so on up to the few top level predators on the cusp of the food web. In this set, diatoms and flagellates are on the bottom and tunas and barracudas at the top. Whale sharks? they eat plankton, like many damselfish.

13. Which of these are marine invertebrate metazoan animals, most with an operculum?

a) starfish
b) bony fish
c) tunicates
d) gastropods

14. "Primary production", the work of plant life, is the foundation of the food web. What are the major primary producers on a coral reef?

a) algal turfs that grow on and around the reefs
b) the vast seagrass beds that grow in the shallow flats
c) *zooxanthellae*
d) the phytoplankton that fill the waters above the reef

15. Which of the following group of fishes are simultaneous hermaphrodites?

a) groupers
b) clownfish
c) gobies
d) hamlets

16. Which is a good example of a reef fish with a pharyngeal mill?

a) surgeonfishes
b) parrotfishes
c) wrasses
d) damselfishes

13. d) The gastropods are the mollusks known generally as snails. Most have a muscular foot that extends out of a coiled shell and provides locomotion. This muscular foot usually has a horny plate, the operculum, that seals the opening of the shell when the foot is retracted. Bony fish also have operculums, the gill cover, but then they are not invertebrates.

14. a) Nutrients are scarce in the waters around a coral reef but primary production is high. Both algal turfs embedded in the reef structure and *zooxanthellae* contribute greatly to primary production on coral reefs, but algal turfs are now thought to be the major source of carbon production in the reef environment.

15. d) There are a number of patterns of sexuality that occur in reef fish, and simultaneous hermaphroditism is one that is not very common. The hamlets, *Hypoplectrus* sp., family Serranidae, are active males and females at the same time. Self fertilization, however, does not occur. An individual can spawn as a female and then a short time later, spawn as male. The pair may then reverse roles a short time later. This ensures that two fish can always spawn without regard to distribution of the sexes.

16. b) Many species of parrotfish are equipped with a formidable pharyngeal apparatus or mill. This modification of the mouth allows the parrotfish, an herbivore, to feed on the turf algae embedded in coral reefs by simply biting into the reef structure, rock and algae together, reducing it all to sand sized grains and pushing the entire mass through the digestive system. The algae is digested and the sand just passes through.

17. The oceans cover

a) half the surface of the earth.

b) two thirds (66%) of the earth's surface.

c) three fourths of the earth's surface.

d) 70.8% of the earth's surface.

18. Which is the best characterization of the anemone and clownfish relationship?

a) opportunism on the part of the clownfish

b) acceptance on the part of the anemone

c) symbiosis, a biological relationship

d) true love

19. What makes seawater salty?

a) Only one major salt, sodium chloride (NaCL), gives the sea its salt.

b) Hundreds of compounds, many of them salts contribute to the density of seawater.

c) Seven major salts are always present in the same ratios in oceanic and coastal seawater.

d) none of the above

20. Phosphate gas, which forms from the interaction between algae and fish feces, is quickly taken up and trapped by the sediments around coral reefs.

a) True, which is why phosphate is so limited in natural sea water.

b) False, the sediments give up phosphate gas.

c) True, phosphate is trapped until the sea floor is exposed by geologic activity.

d) False, total gobbledygook, don't believe a word of it.

17. d) This is a rather precise figure but the earth has an area of abut 196,938,800 square miles and so a tenth of a percent of the area of the earth is about 200,000 square miles, so there is a lot of room for error, even at a tenth of a percent.

18. c) Often, two unrelated species live together in an intimate association that benefits both of the species without causing damage to either partner. The correct term for this type of association is symbiosis. True love is not found between anemones and clownfish because neither species can sing.

19. c) The seven major salts present in seawater are sodium chloride, magnesium chloride, magnesium sulphate, calcium sulfate, potassium sulfate, calcium carbonate and potassium or sodium bromide. They make up 99.5 % of all the conservative elements (salts that are always in the same ratios) in seawater.

20. d) Phosphate does not form gas, the whole concept in this question is chemically preposterous. However, phosphate is incorporated into sediments, phosphate is limited in seawater, and some dissolved phosphate does escape into the air with droplets of water so there is something vaguely familiar in these choices. Guessing can be hazardous.

21. Pangaea is

a) the ancient goddess of coral reefs.

b) a supercontinent 200 million years ago.

c) a genus of flatworms found in reef sediments.

d) a Spanish recipe for fish soup.

22. What is the average depth (mean) of the oceans?

a) about 15 meters (50 feet)

b) about 60 meters (200 feet)

c) about 1 kilometer (0.62 miles)

d) about 4 kilometers (2.5 miles)

23. The Tropic of Cancer (23.5 degrees N) and the Tropic of Capricorn (23.5 degrees S) are two parallels of latitude that define the Torrid Zone on either side of the Equator, the area where most coral reefs occur.

a) True, these were the zones developed by the ancient Greeks that delimited the known world.

b) False, the Tropics of Cancer and Capricorn are just fictional titles from the torrid novels of Henry Miller.

c) True, these are the turning points of the sun.

d) False, The Tropic of Cancer is south and the Tropic of Capricorn is north.

24. What unusual trait do the octopus and flounder have in common?

a) They both have a poisonous bite.

b) They both contain *zooxanthellae*.

c) They both live only in tropical seas.

d) The are both capable of rapid color changes.

21. b) 200 million years ago all the continents of Earth were joined into one large land mass, which was given the name Pangaea by Alfred Wegener in 1912. This supercontinent began to break up into separate continents about 180 million years ago.

22. d) Yeah, that's awful deep, but the oceans are very deep and very large. They make up about 71% of the earth's surface, and the extensive shallow seas are but a very small part of the great expanses of deep oceans.

23. c) The word "tropic" has its origin in from the Latin *tropicus* which comes from the Greek *trope* (turning). The two lines of latitude that are the Tropic of Cancer (N) and the Tropic of Capricorn (S) are the points on the earth at which the sun reaches its zenith at the solstice and then "turns" back to travel the other way.

24. d) Many coral reef animals have coloration that helps them blend in with their background, but few can match the octopus and the flounder in their ability to change their own color patterns to blend in with various backgrounds. Seemingly in the wink of an eye these creatures can change color and pattern to blend in perfectly with a wide variety of substrate colors and patterns. There are many species of octopus and flounder that live in temperate seas.

25. Specific gravity is a measure of the amount of salt dissolved in sea water.

a) True, the more dissolved salt the higher the specific gravity.

b) False, specific gravity only measures density.

c) True, but only if corrected for water temperature.

d) False, specific gravity is a measure of the volume of pure water in the solution.

26. How deep can light penetrate into the oceans?

a) 10 m (33 feet)

b) 680 m (2231 feet)

c) 1000 m (3280 feet)

d) 1609 m (5280 feet)

27. Mimicry, aggressive and defensive, is often found in marine coral reef fishes. Which is a good example of aggressive mimicry?

a) lionfish, *Pterois volitans*

b) saber-toothed mimic blenny, *Aspidontus taeniatus*

c) comet, *Calloplesiops altivelis*

d) Red Sea mimic blenny, *Ecsenius gravieri*

28. In which of the following groups are all three part of the sea plankton?

a) diatoms, copepods, kelp

b) dinoflagellates, *Caulerpa*, rotifers

c) diatoms, copepods, bacteria

d) plastic bags, fish eggs, swimming crabs

25. b) Specific gravity is a measure of density and the density of seawater is determined by salinity, pressure and temperature. Specific gravity is a *ratio* of the weight (density) of saltwater to the weight (density) of pure fresh water. Salinity is the measure of the actual amount of salt in seawater (parts per thousand salt), but salinity can be estimated from specific gravity (density).

26. c) Sunlight does not penetrate below about 1000 m. At this depth, even the faint blue light of the deeps is gone, and the only light is the occasional burst of bio-luminescence from various organisms that can emit their own light.

27. b) Mimicry is the phenomenon where one species closely resembles another species and gains a survival advantage because of this resemblance. There are a number of types of mimicry but probably the best known aggressive mimic is the saber-toothed blenny. This species mimics the cleaner wrasse, *Labroides dimidiatus.* When a large fish comes to be cleaned of parasites, the look alike saber-toothed blenny takes a bite out of the fish instead of picking off parasites. The Red Sea mimic blenny is a passive (Batesian) mimic.

28. c) Plankton is composed of living organisms, small and large, that float freely in the sea unattached to the bottom and that move without much self determination, traveling wherever wind and tidal currents propel them. Man made floating objects are flotsam, not plankton, and large swimming organisms such as sailfish and swimming crabs may inhabit the planktonic realm but are not planktonic creatures.

29. The bright colors of many coral reef fish are termed "poster colors" and function to

a) conceal their presence from predators.

b) notify others of their species of their reproductive status.

c) establish a territory.

d) all of the above

30. Where is the "rubble zone" found?

a) where the grass flats drop to deep water

b) along the edge of reef formations

c) right next to Fred's place

d) in the rocks under the reefs

31. On the reef, some fish and invertebrates have very close associations. Which of the following is not an obligate association between a fish and an invertebrate?

a) clownfish and anemone

b) pearlfish and sea cucumber

c) cardinalfish and queen conch

d) neon goby and tube sponge

32. Plankton is often put into categories by size. From smallest to largest what is the proper order?

a) microplankton, macroplankton, nanoplankton, ultraplankton

b) ultraplankton, nanoplankton, microplankton, macroplankton

c) ultraplankton, microplankton, nanoplankton, macropankton.

d) nanoplankton, ultraplankton, microplankton, macroplankton

29. d) Behavioral scientists think that there are a number of reasons that bright colors have evolved in coral reef fishes and the above three are only a few of these. Certainly concealment and escape from predators (eye masks, and camouflage), species recognition (schooling, territory protection), and reproduction (male/female recognition, spawning readiness) are most important.

30. b) As one approaches reef formations, the remains of dead corals tossed about by storms form a rocky rubble area between the reefs and the grass or sand bottoms, and this is the rubble zone. Actually, Barney never called his place a zone.

31. d) Occasionally, a neon goby may be found in a tube sponge, and there are other species of gobies that are almost always found in tube sponges, but this association is not obligatory, whereas the fish in the other pairs do not exist in nature except within that association.

32. b) This is more of a mathematical than a biological question since the prefixes refer to a measure of size rather than biological function. However, ultraplankton is smaller than 5 microns, nanoplankton is smaller than 60 microns, microplankton is 0.06 to 1 mm, and macroplankton are the largest organisms, larger than 1 mm. Plankton nets are sized to capture the plankton in a particular size range.

33. Which is the most abundant dissolved gas in seawater?

a) oxygen
b) carbon dioxide
c) nitrogen
d) hydrogen sulfide

34. The great ocean trenches are the deepest depths of the oceans. Which is the deepest ocean trench?

a) the Aleutian Trench
b) the Challenger Deep
c) the Philippine Trench
d) the Peru-Chile Trench

35. Where are Trilobites found?

a) ancient rocks of marine origin
b) the starship *Enterprise*
c) some types of live rock from Fiji
d) as a commensal on large sponges

36. Which of the following invertebrates has been known to catch and eat small fish?

a) giant clams
b) brittlestars
c) feather duster worms
d) sea fans

33. c) An easy one. Nitrogen is the most abundant gas in the atmosphere, thus it must also be the most abundant gas dissolved in the sea. Nitrogen gas is present in seawater at about 15 parts per million.

34. b) The Challenger Deep, a portion of the Mariana Trench has a depth of 11,022 meters (6.85 miles) and is the deepest depth in the ocean. The Peru-Chile Trench at 5900 kilometers (9495 miles) is the longest of the ocean trenches. Ocean trenches are usually located on the seaward side of island chains known as island arcs.

35. a) Fossil-bearing rocks of the Cambrian Period (600 million years ago when life was proliferating in ancient seas) contain many species of Trilobites. These early arthropods (probably the first creatures with eyes) are well represented in the early fossil record but have been extinct for 225 million years.

36. b) None of these invertebrates are typically considered to be piscivores (fish eaters), but there is one species of brittlestar, *Ophiarachma incrassata*, that commonly feeds on small fish. It lifts its oral disk above the substrate on all five arms creating a sort of table effect. Then when a small fish goes "under the table" seeking shelter, the brittlestar quickly spirals the oral disk trapping the fish within a helical cylinder of spines.

37. Which is the largest structure made by life on earth?

a) the great wall of China

b) the Amazon rain forest

c) the Great Barrier Reef off Australia

d) the Pacific kelp beds

38. This is a good example of a top level predator in a coral reef ecosystem.

a) tunicate

b) barracuda

c) damselfish

d) tropical fish collector

39. Which of the following groups contains animal species that are very important herbivores on coral reefs.

a) damselfish, basket stars, gorgonians

b) starfish, sponges, bristleworms

c) parrotfish, sea urchins, surgeonfish

d) sea cucumbers, queen conchs, spiny lobsters

40. Where does "marine snow" occur?

a) along the shoreline of Arctic and Antarctic seas

b) in the great ocean depths

c) in the wakes of the great cruise ships

d) This is the precipitation of calcium carbonate over the shallow waters of the Bahama Banks.

37. c) The correct answer, of course, depends on the definition of "structure". In most books and minds, the Great Barrier Reef is the largest structure made by life on earth.

38. b) A top level predator, the highest trophic level, in a particular ecosystem is a predator that has few, if any, animals that prey upon it. In this selection, the barracuda fills this slot. A tropical fish collector also has few predators, a tiger shark perhaps, but the collector is not a natural denizen of that ecosystem.

39. c) There are a number of species in these particular groups of coral reef animals that are important grazers on coral reefs. They each feed on different types of algal growths and function to "clean" the reefs of algae and make it easier for corals to settle and grow on hard, exposed substrate. Note that damselfish, starfish, and spiny lobsters, while important inhabitants of coral reef areas, are carnivores and not herbivores.

40. b) "Marine snow" is the continuous shower of tiny organic particles that orginate in the surface waters and drift down into the great depths of the oceans. These areas are so deep and dark that no plants can grow, so the only source of nutrients is what rains down from the brightly lit surface waters. As it falls, microbes, invertebrates, and fish feed upon it. It is the foundation of the deep sea food chain.

41. Which three organisms are all good examples of zooplankton.

a) krill, copepods, diatoms

b) diatoms, dinoflagellates, copepods

c) larval fish, arrow worm, medusa

d) phylosome larvae, zoea, sargassum

42. Where is a barrier reef located?

a) right on the coastline

b) some distance off the coast

c) around an island

d) near an estuary

43. What happens when a shark is finned?

a) Another shark defends its territory by scraping its fins along the intruders side.

b) It is sold for $5.00.

c) The fins are removed for sale.

d) The male is courting a female.

44. Geologically speaking, the Great Barrier Reef off Australia is

a) a relatively recent development.

b) an ancient reef formation, one of the earliest.

c) the same age as all Pacific coral reefs.

d) a young age to the north and old in the south.

41. c) Zooplankton, of course, refers to the organisms that compose the animal part of the plankton. Phytoplankton are planktonic plants. The only group of three that are all animals is c). Diatoms, dinoflagellates and sargassum are all plants.

42. b) A barrier reef is a long coastal reef that occurs relatively far offshore with a stretch of deep water between the reef and the coast. A fringing reef occurs near the coast, and an atoll forms around a small island.

43. c) Finning is the horrendous practice of catching a shark on hook and line, bringing it up to the side of the boat, cutting off the fins for sale in the Asian markets, and then discarding the rest of the shark, alive or dead. This awful commercial practice destroys the shark for a small economic return and is responsible for a large part of the population decline of this important top predator in the ecosystem of the seas.

44. a) Coral reefs have existed on the north-east continental margin of Australia only for the last two million years, not a long time in the geologic history of the world. This period was characterized by extensive sea level changes causing great erosion of old reefs during exposure and extensive coral growth on old reef beds during emersion.

45. A scyaphilic organism

    a) reproduces by budding.

    b) does not need light to survive.

    c) sheds "dandruff-like" flakes.

    d) grows in a long curved "scythe like" manner.

46. Which composes 3.5 percent of sea water?

    a) nitrogen gas

    b) salts

    c) organic matter

    d) phytoplankton

47. When a fish blends in with its background so well that it is difficult to see, the fish is said to

    a) be masked.

    b) have cryptic coloration.

    c) be cloaked.

    d) have disruptive coloration.

48. What provides direct evidence for the theory of Plate Tectonics, which describes the movement of the continental crustal plates?

    a) a satellite tracking of the movement of small dinner plate sized reflectors on mountain ranges

    b) measurements of the speed of light reflected off the moon from various locations

    c) measuring the increase in tension on transoceanic communications cables

    d) analysis of core samples and magnetic patterns on the seafloor around the oceanic ridges

45. b) A tough question. Not many clues, you have to know that "scyaphilic" means "loves darkness" to be sure of the answer. However, the "philic" part means "loves" so **b)** is the only one that really fits.

46. b) The salinity of seawater varies from about 32 to 37 parts per thousand (1.024 to 1028 sg) . Some areas have higher salinities (the Red Sea at 40 ppt, for example) and many near shore areas have lower salinities. The general average, however is 35 ppt which makes seawater 3.5 percent salt.

47. b) The difference between cryptic coloration and disruptive coloration is that cryptically colored fish blend into the background to the point that they can not be distinguished and disruptively colored fish can be seen but their movement and coloration prevent the predator from getting a "fix" on their position. Only Klingon fish are cloaked.

48. d) In 1965, the R/V *Eltanin* did research that showed that the magnetic patterns in the volcanic rock seafloor were symmetrical on either side of the Pacific-Antarctic ridge, reflecting the even spread of seafloor. And in 1969 the Glomar Challenger drilled core holes on either side of south Atlantic ridge and showed that the Earth's crust became progressively older as the distance increased from the center of the ridge.

49. What is a microhabitat?

a) a restricted set of specific environmental parameters to which a particular organism is adapted

b) an area of the reef less then one square meter

c) an area of any sea bottom less than one square cm

d) a bikini for nuns

50. In nature, a clownfish is a good example of

a) a facultative symbiotic organism.

b) a commensal organism.

c) an obligate symbiotic organism.

d) a biologically supporting organism.

51. What are the three basic types of coral reefs?

a) barrier, patch, spur and groove

b) fringing, atoll, patch

c) atoll, spur and groove, slope

d) fringing, atoll, barrier

52. The Pacific Ocean is getting smaller and the Atlantic Ocean is getting bigger.

a) True, the Coriolis effect moves water into the Atlantic more rapidly so Atlantic water levels are rising faster.

b) False, the ocean basins are static and no changes are now occurring.

c) True, research on the theory of Plate Tectonics demonstrates that the Atlantic basin is expanding and the Pacific basin is shrinking.

d) False, the Atlantic is shrinking and the Pacific is expanding.

49. a) There are many elements that create a "habitat". Food supply, protection from predation and competition, support for reproduction, as well as a defined physical area are the primary elements. Great restriction of any or all of these usually define a microhabitat. A microhabitat refers more to a restricted ecological niche rather than to a restricted physical living space. Please note that there is a great difference between a habitat and a habit.

50. c) In nature, clownfish must associate with an anemone (obligate symbiosis) while an anemone can survive without clownfish (faculative symbosis). A commensal organism lives with, on, or in another organism without injury to that organism. The host of a commensal gains little from the association. In the case of the clownfish/anemone association, the clownfish gains protection, and the anemone may gain protection from coral eating fish and some tactile stimulation.

51. d) A fringing reef forms a border along the shore and is an extension of the coastline structure. Patch reefs and spur and groove formations are structures often found in fringing reefs. Barrier reefs are far from shore with a lagoon or wide channel separating the reef and the coast. Atoll reefs are circular, usually with a central lagoon or island, and are formed as an island slowly sinks beneath the sea.

52. c) Geological research along the mid ocean ridges has shown that over the last 150 million years, the movement of the continents over Earth's mantle has steadily expanded the Atlantic and shrunk the Pacific.

53. Why are sponges often found in deep overhangs and caves in coral reefs?

a) Water currents sweep more strongly through and under reef structures.

b) Many sponges do not require intense lighting and can not compete with algae in areas where light is intense.

c) Currents are slower in these areas and sponges can better capture planktonic organisms.

d) Downward growth is easier than upward growth.

54. A colonial ascidian can easily be mistaken for a

a) coral.

b) sponge.

c) gorgonian.

d) queue at the post office.

55. Why is the sea blue?

a) Seawater transmits blue light most easily.

b) Blue light is absorbed by seawater.

c) Centuries of pollution have made it unhappy.

d) Because of reflection and back scattering.

56. Why are natural marine refugia a very good concept.

a) It puts the sump to good use.

b) It produces food for fish and invertebrates.

c) It protects a natural adult reproductive stock that will then seed other areas.

d) It gives our military a chance for some R & R.

53. b) High intensity light stimulates lush algal growth and this can overgrow and kill sponges and corals. Areas that receive less light offer less algal competition to sponge growth.

54. b) There are many kinds of colonial ascidians (tunicates). Some are brightly colored in reds, yellows, and greens, and some are black and grey. Some species have amorphous, globular growth patterns and look very much like sponges, but their firm cellulose-like tunica (composed of a carbohydrate, tunicin) and twin openings of incurrent and excurrent siphons soon reveal them to be colonial tunicates.

55. d) Blue light is most readily reflected from the sea surface and it also penetrates most deeply, thus contributes most to back scattering from submerged particles. The greenish shallow inshore waters get their color from broad spectrum light scattering, suspended micro algae, and bottom colors. Brown and yellow waters get color from the sediments they carry.

56. c) The concept of a natural marine refugia is to create reserves of large natural marine areas where no fishing or consumptive uses of any type are allowed. This will protect breeding areas and allow populations of fish and invertebrates to gain maximum reproductive capacity, which will provide continuous seed for populations in other exploited areas. Such refugia may prevent the collapse of heavily exploited fish stocks, such as the cod fisheries off New England.

57. Which oceanic area has the greatest natural salinity.

a) The Caribbean
b) The Red Sea
c) The Indo-Pacific
d) The Gulf of Mexico

58. Which three are good examples of organisms that compose the nekton of the sea.

a) sargassum rafts, jellyfish, fish eggs
b) copepods, jellyfish, larval fish
c) flying fish, squid, whale shark
d) krill, penguins, iceberg

59. Which of the following group of fishes are almost all gonochoristic (fish with separate sexes throughout life)?

a) groupers
b) clownfish
c) gobies
d) hamlets

60. Although nutrients are tightly cycled within a coral reef, there are outside sources of nutrient input. These outside nutrient sources include

a) fish feces.
b) deep water upwellings.
c) plankton.
d) all of the above.

57. b) The Red Sea with an average salinity of 37 to 42 ppt has the highest oceanic salinity. The salinity of enclosed, shallow, near shore areas can climb to above 60 ppt, but the average oceanic salinity is 34 to 36 ppt (1.0252 to 1.0268).

58. c) The nekton are those animals that live in the open sea but control their own movement and migrations by swimming significant distances. The organisms of the plankton, on the other hand, are dependent on water currents for their movement through the sea.

59. c) The gobies are a vast and varied family of fishes. Almost all, however, are gonochoristic (separate sexes). Neon gobies, *Gobiosoma oceanops,* for example, are strict gonochorists. Recently, however, a few species of gobies in the genus *Coryphopterus*, have been shown to be sequential (protogynous) hermaphrodites, so sexuality may be more versatile in this vast family.

60. d) Although the waters around coral reefs are generally very nutrient poor, there are other sources of nutrients that enter coral reefs. Since most corals are predators and consume planktonic organisms, the plankton that flows through coral reefs imports nutrients to the reef. Even the fecal pellets from fish that feed off the reef at night and rest over the corals during the day contribute nutrients to the corals. Seasonal upwellings of deep, nutrient laden water also import nutrients.

61. Choanocytes are cells that make up most of the living tissue of which group of animals?

  a) starfish

  b) tunicates

  c) sponges

  d) gastropods

62. The symmetry of corals and anemones is

  a) bilateral.

  b) amorphous.

  c) radial.

  d) eight tentacled.

63. Which of the phyla listed below, is the phylum composed of animals that occur only in marine waters ?

  a) molluska

  b) Arthropoda

  c) Platyhelminthes

  d) Echinodermata

64. The length of the tidal day, which is the period of one complete tidal cycle, is

  a) just like the earth's rotation, twenty four hours.

  b) less than the earth's rotation, 23 hours, 10 minutes.

  c) more than the earth's rotation, 24 hours, 50 minutes.

  d) half the earth's rotation, 12 hours.

61. c) Sponges have very few cell types. Choanocytes are the cells that bear a flagellum and serve to move water through the body of the sponge. The amoebocytes are the cells that have pseudopodia (moveable projections of cell cytoplasm) and that take up food particles, digest them and move the nutrients throughout the sponge.

62. c) Corals and anemones are round in horizontal cross section without a dorsal or ventral surface, thus their symmetry is radial. They have neither a right nor left side, but they do have up and down ends.

63. d) The echinoderms (starfish, sea urchins, sea cucumbers, and brittle stars) occur only in marine waters; the other phyla: clams and snails, crabs and shrimp, and flatworms also occur in freshwater and some are terrestrial as well.

64. c) The moon moves along in its orbit in the same direction as the earth revolves, but not at the same speed. To bring the moon to the same spot over the earth as it was 24 hours ago, the moon must move an additional 12 degrees, which takes 50 minutes longer. Thus the crest of the high lunar tide (the peak height of the bulge in the earth's oceans caused by the gravitational pull of the moon) is 50 minutes later each day. The water bulge on the side of the earth opposite the moon, the cause of the second high tide in each day, is the result of the centrifugal forces created by the rotation of earth and moon around a common point (the barycenter). Low tides are the troughs between these "bulges".

65. In which group of organisms listed below are all three members of the epifauna of the reef?

 a) barracuda, squid, moon jellyfish

 b) bristle worm, tunicate, boring sponge

 c) cleaner shrimp, anemone, flame scallop

 d) sea urchin, sea walnut, sea biscuit

66. All species of corals grow very slowly.

 a) True, because some large coral heads are thousands of years old.

 b) False, although many massive corals grow slowly, some branching corals exhibit relatively rapid growth.

 c) True, this is why coral reefs are limited in size.

 d) False, corals grow rapidly, it is just their massive size that makes it seem like slow growth.

67. Most coral reef fish produce very tiny larvae that live as planktonic organisms. What is the typical length of planktonic larval life for these fishes?

 a) one week

 b) six weeks

 c) three weeks

 d) three months

68. Which of the following group of fish are protanderous hermaphrodites (male first, female second)?

 a) groupers

 b) clownfish

 c) gobies

 d) hamlets

65. c) The epifauna (epi - upon, on, at, over, near; fauna - animals) of the reef are those animals that live on and among the structures of the reef. This does not include those that live in the plankton over the reef or deep in the sediments of the reef (the infauna). Only all three of the animals in c) live on or among the reef structure. At least one member of all the other groups lives above the reef or within the rocks and sediments of the reef.

66. b) There are many species of corals and there are many different modes and rates of growth. Massive coral heads grow very slowly, but branching corals (*Acropora* sp.,for example) and soft corals grow relatively rapidly when conditions are good for growth and development.

67. c) Of course there is great variation of the term of larval life within a species and between species, but in general, most coral reef fish spend about 3 weeks as planktonic larvae before becoming juveniles.

68. b) The term protanderous means "male first". Fishes with this pattern of sexuality mature first as males and then become females when stimulated by the proper social interactions with other fish of the same species. Clownfish are excellent examples of protanderous hermaphroditism. Two to five young clownfish will almost always develop a male/female pair or two as they mature.

69. The most important source of nutrients for hermatypic corals is

a) fish feces

b) *zooxanthellae*

c) plankton

d) water borne nutrients

70. Which species is a good example of Batesian mimicry?

a) lionfish, *Pterois volitans*

b) saber-toothed mimic blenny, *Aspidontus taeniatus*

c) comet, *Calloplesiops altivelis*

d) Red Sea mimic blenny, *Ecsenius gravieri*

71. What are Kuroshio, Agulhas, and Labrador?

a) islands in the Pacific Ocean

b) islands in the Atlantic Ocean

c) major wind driven ocean currents

d) reef formations in the Caribbean Sea

72. The unusual embryonic development of the Atlantic sand shark, *Carcharias taurus*, and the mako and thresher sharks includes oophagy. What is oophagy?

a) The mother releases the eggs and eats them and development is completed in mother's digestive system.

b) The developing embryos feed upon newly released eggs within the uterus for some time before birth.

c) The embryos are nourished within the uterus by secretions from the uterine wall.

d) The delivery of digestive gasses into the uterus supplies nutrients to the embryos.

69. b) Despite their structural simplicity, corals
are complex animals and can gain nutrients from a
variety of sources. Probably the most important
nutrient source for hermatypic corals, those that have
zooxanthellae within their tissues, are the nutrients that
these algal cells produce through photosynthesis.

70. d) Batesian mimicry (named after the English
naturalist Henry W. Bates) is the term used when a
harmless species mimics a species that is harmful or
distasteful to predators. The Red Sea mimic blenny is
seldom attacked by predators because it closely
resembles the black-lined saber-toothed blenny,
Meiacanthus nigrovittatus, which gives would be
predators a venomous bite.

71. c) The major ocean currents are driven by
seasonally stable wind patterns that circle the Earth.
The Kuroshio Current is off Japan, the Agulhas
Current is off South Africa, and the Labrador Current
is in the North Atlantic.

72. b) The feeding of developing shark embryos
on recently released eggs within the uterus is most
advanced in the gray nurse sharks. Here the most
advanced embryos actually hunt the less developed
embryos in the uterus and consume them. Only one
embryo per uterine horn is produced. Evidently the
concept of brotherly love takes on a very different
meaning for grey nurse shark siblings.

73. There is a designation of plankton termed the "holoplankton". This refers to planktonic organisms

a) without joints.

b) with holes in their structure.

c) that have both plant and animal characteristics.

d) that spend their entire lives within the plankton.

74. What causes the great water flows known as tides?

a) the wind patterns that circle the Earth

b) the great conflict between Neptune and Poseidon

c) the gravitational forces of both sun and moon

d) the gravitational force of the moon

75. The terms massive, columnar, encrusting, branching, foliaceous, laminar, and free living refer to

a) the growth patterns of sponges.

b) the growth patterns of algae.

c) the activities of marine science students on spring break.

d) the growth patterns of corals.

76. Which of the following group of fish are protogynous hermaphrodites?

a) groupers

b) clownfish

c) gobies

d) hamlets

73. d) There are many different categories of plankton. The opposite of holoplankton (most copepods and phytoplankton, for example) is meroplankton, which includes those planktonic organisms that are developmental stages (eggs and larvae) of organisms that leave the plankton once that development stage is completed.

74. c) Tidal currents are complex because they are affected by winds (centrifugal and centripetal forces), inertia, and water movements between oceans and seas. Because it is so far away, the tidal-raising force of the sun is only 46% that of the moon, but it is the gravitational force of both the sun and moon that create the tides.

75. d) Various species of corals grow in almost every conceivable pattern. The possible growth patterns are determined basically by genetics, but environmental conditions provide the stimulus for the particular growth pattern that is expressed.

76. a) The term protogynous means "female first" (proto - first, gynous - female). Fishes with this pattern of sexuality mature first as females and then after functioning as a female for one to many seasons, some large females stimulated by social interactions, change into functioning males and remain so for the rest of their lives. The numbers of males may vary from 2% (heavily exploited populations) to about 20% (relatively unexploited populations).

77. Which group is composed of marine metazoan animals without a nervous system, muscles, or internal organs?

   a) starfish

   b) sponges

   c) tunicates

   d) gastropods

78. Sharks are evil and cruel predators.

   a) True, they will eat almost anything.

   b) False, they are just top level predators.

   c) True, they have no moral conscience.

   d) False, they kill their prey quickly so it won't suffer.

79. The southern stargazer, *Astroscopus y-graecum*, is capable of producing an electric discharge of as much as

   a) 10 volts

   b) 2 volts

   c) 50 volts

   d) 150 volts

80. When do stony corals spawn?

   a) always on the full moon closest to April 1

   b) Each species spawns on a separate month to avoid larval competition in finding a suitable substrate.

   c) The largest coral heads spawn several days before the smaller ones.

   d) Stony corals in various areas are somehow able to synchronize spawning and all spawn at the same time each year.

77. b) Sponges are the "simplest" of multicelled animals in that they lack the diverse cells and tissues that make up other metazoan animals. They are not "primitive", however, in the sense that they are ancestral to other animals, since present day sponges have evolved over eons of time from early sponge species.

78. b) Far too often we humans make the assumption that all of nature reflects the cultural and behavioral characteristics that make us uniquely human. Animals cannot be evil and cruel or kind and loving with the same understanding of their actions that humans possess. They act only through instinct, natural learning, or domestic training by humans. The actions of wild animals are motivated only by survival.

79. c) The southern stargazer typically lies buried in sandy areas with only the fringes on the dorsally oriented mouth exposed. These delicate projections wave in the water and attract small fish, and when the prey gets close enough, the stargazer stuns it with an electrical discharge of up to 50 volts (a good jolt for a marine fish) from the two electrogenic organs located just behind the eyes. Freshwater electric eels can generate voltages of up to 550 volts.

80. d) All large reef building corals in certain areas spawn at the same time each year. On the Great barrier Reef spawning occurs at the full moon in November and off western Australia it occurs in April, In the Caribbean, spawning occurs in late August and/or September.

Marine
Miscellany

Marine Miscellany

In the broadest sense, the world of marine aquariums covers a vast expanse. It includes the twelve year old kid with a 20 gallon aquarium, the public aquarium with tanks that hold half a million gallons, and everything in-between. It is a great and varied assemblage. There are professional marine aquarists that work in large, and not so large, public aquariums, as well as in research laboratories, marine aquaculture hatcheries, retail stores, wholesale establishments, and also as collectors of ornamental marine life. And then there are the hobbyists, the driving force of the industry. Most marine aquarists keep but one or two small tanks, 50 gallons or less, but there are many who have tanks in their living rooms that rival or surpass those of public aquariums.

There is a lot of miscellany associated with this vast industry/hobby. This includes history, people, public aquariums, hobbyist associations, things of marine science and technology, and fascinating information on the creatures of reef and sea. This last section taps into this broad world and will give you a feel for the larger sphere that surrounds the marine aquarium hobby. You may be totally lost on some of the questions, but others may allow you to tap into some specialized domain of knowledge you may possess and easily come up with the right answer. What ever your background and participation in this hobby/industry/science may be, we think you will broaden your knowledge of this world through this little interrogatory exercise.

1. **Which fish is a "quick change artist?**

   a) the orchid dottyback, *Pseudochromis fridmani*
   b) the porcupinefish, *Diodon histrix*
   c) the queen triggerfish, *Balistes vetula*
   d) the peacock flounder, *Bothus lunatus*

2. **Large aquariums live in fear of spalling. What is this condition?**

   a) the spread of visitors into unauthorized areas
   b) the bowing outward of aquarium glass or plastic
   c) the rusting of iron supports within a concrete structure resulting in expansion and cracking
   d) groups of visitors singing to the fish in off key tones that cause stress to fish and other visitors

3. **MASNA is the acronym for**

   a) Marine Aquarium Stores for Native Animals.
   b) Menfolk Actively Seeking New Acropora.
   c) Marine Aquarists Society for National Action.
   d) Marine Aquarium Societies of North America.

4. **Who first described the spawning behavior of pygmy angelfish, *Centropyge* sp.?**

   a) Ronald Thresher
   b) John Randall
   c) Joe and Sally Bauer
   d) Scott Michael

1. d) Flounders, especially the peacock flounder, have the amazing ability to rapidly blend in with the background colors of the sea bottom. Dark, light, or speckled, the flounder somehow senses the color and pattern of the bottom and changes the color of its upper side to blend in so well that it becomes virtually invisible.

2. c) Modern concrete aquariums are now built with fiberglass supports and improved concrete formulas and for the most part spalling does not occur in tank walls. It can be a major problem for older aquariums, however, and requires costly repair.

3. d) In this modern age, there are many reasons for marine aquarists, through their local societies, to interact and combine efforts. Protection of the hobby, dissemination of accurate information, and coordination of activities are some of the major reasons. MASNA, now a confederation of about 28 societies, was formed to provide an interactive structure for marine aquarium societies. MASNA also coordinates the annual MACNA conference.

4. c) Joe and Sally Bauer, both physicians, were ardent marine aquarium hobbyists in the 1970's, founding the Cleveland Saltwater Enthusiasts Association, CSEA. In addition to being one of the first hobbyists to rear clownfish, they made extensive observations on the spawning behavior of pygmy angelfish, publishing their results in 1981 in a scientific journal, The Bulletin of Marine Science.

5. Why do the royal dottyback, *Pseudochromis paccagnellae*, and the royal gramma, *Gramma loreto*, have nearly identical coloration of royal purple anteriorly and golden yellow posteriorly?

  a) the expression of similar ancestral genes

  b) a classic example of convergent evolution

  c) beats me

  d) a case of mimicry

6. Who developed the copper treatment for parasites of marine fish?

  a) George Blasiola

  b) Nelson Herwig

  c) Robert Dempster

  d) John Gratzek

7. Which of these fish is a sponge eater?

  a) the orchid dottyback, *Pseudochromis fridmani*

  b) the exquisite butterflyfish, *Chaetodon austriacus*

  c) the threadfin butterflyfish, *Chaetodon auriga*

  d) the French angelfish, *Pomacanthus paru*

8. This is the longest continuously active public aquarium in the United States.

  a) The John G. Shedd Aquarium

  b) The New York Aquarium, Brooklyn, NY

  c) Steinhart Aquarium

  d) Steven Birch Aquarium-Museum

5. b) The appearance of an animal: coloration, form, size, etc., although based in its genetic code, is a result of environmental forces acting on the gene pool of the species over vast periods of time. Occasionally, relatively unrelated animals in totally different areas assume the same coloration and form because, in part, they occupy similar ecological niches. This is called convergent evolution.

6. c) All of these gentlemen have made important contributions to our understanding and control of fish disease, but it was Robert Dempster at the Steinhart Aquarium who published the article, "The Use of Copper Sulfate as a Cure for Fish Diseases Caused by Parasitic Dinoflagellates of the Genus *Oodinium*" in the journal *Zoologica* in 1955. Since that paper was written, the genus for the marine form of the parasite has been changed from *Oodinium* to *Amyloodinium*.

7. d) In nature, the French angelfish and the Grey (or Black) angelfish, *P. arcuatus*, among others, feed primarily on sponges, algae and reef detritus. In captivity, they usually learn to eat ordinary aquarium foods and typically do very well in aquaria. Older specimens seem to have a more difficult time adjusting to aquarium environments than young ones, a generalization that holds true for many species.

8. b) The New York Aquarium first opened in 1896 and operated at the original location at the southwest tip of Manhattan until 1910. The aquarium then moved to Coney Island, NY and now draws over 750,000 visitors per year.

9. Which of these fish is a coral eater?

  a) the orchid dottyback, *Pseudochromis fridmani*
  b) the exquisite butterflyfish, *Chaetodon austriacus*
  c) the threadfin butterflyfish, *Chaetodon auriga*
  d) the French angelfish, *Pomacanthus paru*

10. Who was the first to rear French angelfish from the egg?

  a) Frank Hoff
  b) Stormy Mayo
  c) Martin Moe
  d) Barbara Palko

11. What can be either centric, pennate, or both in a marine aquarium?

  a) brown algae
  b) sponges
  c) diatoms
  d) crabs

12. Which are the smallest adult crabs?

  a) the swimming crabs of the sargassum weed
  b) pea crabs
  c) ghost crabs
  d) hermit crabs

9. b) There are many species of butterflyfish and many of these enter the marine ornamental trade even though they are ill suited to life in an aquarium. Many, such as the exquisite and the ornate butterflyfish, *C. Ornatissimus*, feed on corals. Others, however, such as the threadfin butterflyfish, do very well in aquaria. It is very important for the marine aquarist to know the characteristics of each fish before purchase as this will save money and fish and greatly reduce stress for the aquarist.

10. d) Barbara Palko was a fishery biologist with the NOAA Southeast Fisheries Center in Miami. She was working with larval fishes in the early 1970's and collected several French angelfish eggs in the plankton. She succeeded in rearing them to the juvenile stage on wild plankton. In the late 1970's, Martin Moe (me) was the first to commercially rear French and grey angelfish from artificially spawned adults.

11. c) The diatoms, Bacillariophyta, are microscopic photosynthetic algae, single celled and colonial, that are encased in two valved, silica frustules or shells. There are two major groups, centric (round) and pennate (elongate). The frustules are intricately sculpted and the cells are a beautiful golden brown. They may often cover the surfaces of new aquariums with a light brown slime.

12. b) The pea crabs, Pinnotheridae, live inside the shells of mussels and clams and some tunicates. They do not damage the living mollusk, but they do share the food that the mollusk gathers. They are as small as a quarter of an inch (6.3 mm) across the carapace.

13. Which fish exhibits very shocking behavior?

a) the orchid dottyback, *Pseudochromis fridmani*

b) the porcupinefish, *Diodon histrix*

c) the stargazer, *Astroscopus y-graecum*

d) the queen triggerfish, *Balistes vetula*

14. Where is the famous "Ring of Fire" Aquarium located?

a) Monterey, California

b) Osaka, Japan

c) Sydney, Australia

d) Honolulu, Hawaii

15. What is one of the great inventions of the last half century that has made modern aquaristics possible.

a) artificial sea salts

b) the airplane

c) PVC pipe

d) fluorescent lighting

16. This aquarium is affiliated with the world renowned Scripps Institution of Oceanograpy.

a) The John G. Shedd Aquarium

b) Theater of the Sea

c) Steinhart Aquarium

d) Steven Birch Aquarium-Museum

13. c) The stargazer has the unusual ability to release an electric shock from the two electrogenic plates that are located just behind the upward gazing eyes (hence the name "stargazer"). The stargazer buries just under the sand and lures a small fish to the vicinity with the feathery fringes around its mouth. When the target fish is close enough, the stargazer releases a charge of up to 50 volts, stunning the fish just long enough to collect dinner.

14. b) The "Ring of Fire" refers to the active volcanic regions that ring the Pacific Ocean. The theme of the Osaka Aquarium is the life of the Pacific Ocean, from the Arctic to the great tropical environs. The huge, 1.3 million gallon, central tank is in the shape of a Maltese cross and holds two whale sharks as well as at least 50 other species of pelagic fishes. It has probably the greatest annual attendance of any public aquarium.

15. c) Probably more than any other development, non toxic PVC piping made it possible to easily and inexpensively build the infrastructures that makes it possible to move fresh and saltwater to, within, and out of aquarium systems. Artificial sea salts have been around in one form or another since the 19th century.

16. d) The Steven Birch Aquarium is not huge, but has a high caliber of marine displays and works closely with the scientists at Scripps Institution. They pump seawater directly from the Pacific Ocean and make this water available to local marine aquarists.

17. How do whale sharks, those massive plankton feeders of the open ocean, reproduce?

    a) similar to dolphins, production of one large pup born each year

    b) oviparity, like rays, laying eggs that attach to the ocean bottom and eventually well formed young hatch

    c) production of many small pelagic eggs

    d) ovoviviparity, the mother holds the developing eggs within her body and then gives birth to viable young

18. The "Sulfur Pearl of Namibia", *Thiomargarita namibiensis*, is a newly discovered small organism, about 200 microns in diameter. What is it?

    a) a bacteria

    b) an algae

    c) a jellyfish

    d) a copepod

19. Which is the mollusk with the poison dart?

    a) the tulip snail, *Fasciolaria tulipa*

    b) the hairy triton, *Cymatium pileare*

    c) the knobby scallop, *Chlamys imbricata*

    d) the geographic cone, *Conus geographus*

20. This is the best general book on marine aquariums.

    a) *Natural Reef Aquariums* by John Tullock

    b) *The Conscientious Marine Aquarist* by Bob Fenner

    c) *The Marine Aquarium Reference* by Martin Moe

    d) *Dynamic Aquaria* by Walter Adey and Karen Loveland

17. d) Although the details of whale shark reproduction are not well known, the evidence strongly suggests that they are ovoviviparous. The few small, "new born" whale sharks that have been taken were found in the mid Pacific over 10,000 feet of water and thousands of miles from shore. They had a small scar between the pelvic fins where the pseudoumbilicus, a tube between yolk sac and developing embryo, was attached. Dolphins are viviparous mammals with internal fertilization and development of a placenta.

18. a) 200 microns, one fifth of a millimeter, is very small, but for a single celled bacteria, it is enormous. This is one of the largest bacteria known and was discovered in ocean dredgings in the South Atlantic Ocean off the coast of Namibia. It metabolizes sulfur and nitrate and forms chain-like colonies that glow like pearls from the absorbed nitrates.

19. d) Many of the cone shells, there are 400 to 500 species, carry a dangerous toxin. The radula, the rasping teeth of many snails, is modified into little "harpoons" that the cone can shoot into its prey. The geographic cone is very poisonous and is responsible for the deaths of a number of people.

20. a,b,c,d) Oh no, I'm not going to stick my neck out on this one, all the answers are correct! There are many things in science and philosophy that are a matter of opinion and in this case, the "best" book is a matter of choice. All books have their strengths and their weaknesses and marine aquarium books are no different. These are all good books and there are many, many more as well.

21. Discovery of organisms new to science is not unusual, uncommon in these days, but not unusual. However, discovery of a new Phylum is highly unusual. It is quite possible that *Symbion pandora* will prove to represent a new phylum, Cycliophora. This organism was recently found

   a) in a sponge on a Caribbean reef.

   b) between the teeth of a sperm whale.

   c) on the "lips" of a lobster.

   d) around the hydrothermal deep sea vents.

22. Breeding the chambered nautilus is an exceptional achievement. Where was this first accomplished?

   a) National Aquarium in Baltimore

   b) Waikiki Aquarium in Hawaii

   c) Aomori Prefectural Asamushi Aquarium in Japan

   d) Monterey Bay Aquarium in California

23. Who "introduced" reef tanks to the new world?

   a) Tom Frakes

   b) George Smit

   c) Julian Sprung

   d) Albert Thiel

24. This was the year of the first expedition to tropical seas for the purpose of collection of marine tropical fish for aquarium display.

   a) 1861

   b) 1900

   c) 1938

   d) 1950

Answers

21. c) Peter Funch and Reinhardt Kristensen of the University of Copenhagen discovered this tiny animal in late 1995 on the mouth parts of the Norwegian lobster. It was originally thought to be a type of rotifer. It is only about 300 microns long, but it has a complex life history including male, female, and asexual reproductive capacity. The name *Symbion pandora* refers to its symbiotic life with the lobster and the species name alludes to its complex life history, a biological "Pandora's box".

22. b) Scientists and aquarists at the Waikiki Aquarium were able to trap chambered nautilus in chicken wire traps at depths of 300 to 1000 feet and slowly raise them to the surface. The nautilus adapted to life in aquaria and the aquarists were able to create the conditions necessary for them to spawn and for the offspring to survive.

23. b) As with most technologies, the development of modern reef aquariums is a result of many people working together over time. The roots of the "reef aquarium" branch of the hobby, however, began with a series of articles by George Smit in Freshwater and Marine Aquarium Magazine in the mid 1980's.

24. a) Yeah, way back in 1861. William Damon and Albert S. Bickmore, under the direction of P.T. Barnum, sailed a small fishing boat from Bermuda with over 600 tropical marine fishes for display at Barnum's American Museum in New York. Damon is also said to be the first in America to keep a marine aquarium in his home.

25. Why is the MAC very important to the marine aquarium hobby?

   a) The Marine Aquarium Council, an organization composed of environmental, industry, and hobby interests, strives to protect and better the marine aquarium hobby.

   b) Smaller than a Big Mac, the MAC is more suited to quick snacks during aquarium maintenance tasks.

   c) The Marine Aqua Center provides marine aquarists with quick information if problems occur.

   d) *The Marine Aquarium Companion* is an old book that provides excellent advice for new and experienced aquarists.

26. Which is the largest crustacean known?

   a) deep sea giant squid

   b) Japanese spider crab

   c) Alaskan king crab

   d) deep sea isopod

27. Who was the first to commercially breed clownfish?

   a) Bill Addison

   b) Frank Hoff

   c) Joe Lichtenbert

   d) Martin Moe

28. What is a tsunami?

   a) a type of aquarium filter

   b) a new style of aquarium system

   c) a very great wave

   d) a very intense typhoon

25. a) Because the modern marine aquarium hobby depends on wild collections for most of the fish and invertebrates in the trade, the industry and hobby is experiencing conflicts and difficulties associated with collection and transport of specimens. The Marine Aquarium Council was formed to "ensure a sustainable future for the marine aquarium industry, organisms and habitat through market incentives that encourage and support quality and sustainable practices". Marine aquarists are encouraged to support MAC.

26. b) There are many large species of spider crabs, but the Japanese spider crab, *Macrocheira kaempferi*, is the biggest. The largest one found measured 12 feet, 1.5 inches (3.7 m) across the front claws, longer than many automobiles. I have known squids, of course, and they are no crustaceans.

27. d) Yep, this is one first I can claim. I started rearing clownfish back in the fall of 1972 in the garage of my home in St. Petersburg, Florida. I had recently been successful in spawning and rearing pompano for a commercial firm, and in my spare time as a Phd. graduate student I dabbled in clownfish culture. The knowledge I had accumulated with pompano was useful and I soon had hundreds of little clownfish that I began selling to shops and wholesalers.

28. c) Tsunamis are very great oceanic waves that are generated by earthquakes, volcanic eruptions, or vast mud slides on the ocean bottom. These waves, also called seismic sea waves, can travel great distances at hundreds of miles an hour and can reach heights of over 250 feet when they near shore.

29. What is the reproductive mode of the coelacanth, *Latimeria chalumnae*, the lobe fined "living fossil" fish found off the coast of South Africa?

   a) similar to dolphins, production of one large pup, born each year

   b) oviparity, like rays, laying eggs that attach to the ocean bottom with eventual hatching of the young

   c) oophagy, where the young feed on eggs and other embryos within the uterus before birth

   d) ovoviviparity, the mother holds the developing eggs within her body and then gives birth to viable young

30. Who wrote the classic 1959 marine aquarium book, *The Salt Water Aquarium in the Home?*

   a) Dr. Herbert Axelrod

   b) Ross Socolof

   c) Robert Straughan

   d) Dr. William T. Innes

31. Which of these fish is an excavation engineer?

   a) the yellowhead jawfish, *Opisthognathous aurifrons*

   b) the stargazer, *Astroscopus y-graecum*

   c) the spotfin flying fish, *Cypselurus furcatus*

   d) the remora, *Echenesis naucrates*

32. An anemone can't jump and swim!

   a) True, these are sessile animals that move slowly.

   b) False, on the full moon, anemones jump and swim.

   c) True, no anemone has the ability of rapid movement.

   d) False, there is at least one anemone that can avoid predators with relatively rapid swimming motion.

29. d) There has been recent controversy on the reproductive mode of the coelacanth. Oophagy has been reported in several publications, but the work of Heemstra & Compagno (1989) and Hemstra and Greenwood (1992) has shown conclusively that oophagy does not take place and that these fish are purely ovoviviparous. The 9 mm diameter egg produces a viable pup without intrauterine cannibalism or placental development.

30. c) The modern marine aquarium hobby really started in the mid 1950's. Robert Straughan had an aquarium shop in Miami at this time and was also an early collector and shipper of marine fish caught in the Florida Keys. He also published a small magazine, Salt Water Aquarium Magazine, and his book, first published in 1959, went through two editions and numerous printings.

31. a) The jawfish builds deep burrows (for its size) in rubble and sand zones near the reefs. It takes up mouthfuls of sand and fine gravel and spits them out around the burrow. The sides of the burrow are supported with larger pebbles, and it even uses one large pebble to close up the burrow at night. Yellowhead jawfish hover above the burrow during the day feeding on plankton that passes over their site.

32. d) The North Sea anemone, *Stromphia japonica*, can avoid predation by jumping and then swimming for about 6 to 9 feet (2 to3 m). Very unusual behavior for an anemone.

33. Ethology is the study of

   a) reef structure.

   b) the ethics of ecology.

   c) marine ecology.

   d) animal behavior.

34. The animal phylum Placoza, simplest of animals, is found only in marine aquaria.

   a) True, this unique organism was a result of genetic engineering, genes from a coral were inserted into a sponge and a new, man made phylum of animals was created.

   b) False, Come on, you expect us to believe this?

   c) True, *Trichoplax adhaerens*, the only species in this phylum, was first discovered in 1883.

   d) False, the Placoza are just simple sponges.

35. Crepuscular is a term used for a fish that

   a) produces large, active larvae.

   b) is larger than one would expect for its species and age.

   c) is active during periods of low light.

   d) has red blood cells that creep very slowly through blood vessels. (found in some Antartic fishes)

36. Who is the "clownfish lady"?

   a) Arline Addison

   b) Sally Bauer

   c) Barbara Moe

   d) Joyce Wilkerson

33. d) The term Ethology was coined by the French zoologist, Geoffroy Saint-Hilaire. It is the study of animal behavior with emphasis on behavioral patterns that occur in natural environments. This is one area where marine aquarists can contribute observations on behavior of fish and invertebrates, particularly in reef tanks where the captive environment is somewhat similar to the natural environment. The behavior of many animals relatively common in reef tanks may not be well known to science.

34. c) Yep, *Trichoplax adhaerens* was discovered on the walls of a marine aquarium in Austria in 1883 and has never been found except in marine aquaria with rocks and organisms from coral reef areas. It is a very small, amoeba-like animal composed of a few thousand ciliated cells. It reproduces from egg and sperm.

35. c) A diurnal fish is active during the day, a nocturnal fish is active at night, and a crepuscular fish (or invertebrate) is most active during periods of low light, the twilight hours that occur at dusk and dawn. Note that some species of the mostly Antartic family Nototheniidae, the cod icefishes, live at temperatures below freezing and do not have any red blood cells or hemoglobin, and certainly no "creepy" cells.

36. d) Although all of these attractive and interesting women could qualify for this title, Joyce Wilkerson, author of *Clownfishes*, Microcosm, Ltd, is certainly the first lady of clownfishes.

37. Who was the first to sexually reproduce corals in captivity?

   a) Steve Tyree

   b) Lee Chin Eng

   c) Thomas W. Vaughan

   d) Prof. Jean Jaubert

38. On some Indo-Pacific reefs, dynamite is used to collect marine aquarium fish.

   a) True, the fish that are not killed are collected for the marine life trade.

   b) False, although marine food fish have often, tragically, been collected in this manner, ornamentals are not.

   c) True, but only in the Philippines.

   d) False, old stocks of WWII ordinance are used, not dynamite.

39. Which fish is most expandable?

   a) the orchid dottyback, *Pseudochromis fridmani*

   b) the porcupinefish, *Diodon histrix*

   c) the queen triggerfish, *Balistes vetula*

   d) the French angelfish, *Pomacanthus paru*

40. Who was the first to commercially breed dottybacks, *Pseudochromis* sp.

   a) Bill Addison

   b) Robert Brons

   c) Martin Moe

   d) Mark Wilson

37. c) Surprise! Rob Toonen researched the literature and found that Thomas Wayland Vaughan did a study on the corals of the Tortugas in 1908-1915 (published in 1916) and spawned and reared 5 species of corals (*Astrangia solitaria, Favia fraqum, Agaricia purpurea, Porites clavaria,* and *Porites asteroides*). He even kept two species alive from larval settlement to 5 years, some with growth up to 10 cm in diameter. A remarkable accomplishment given the primitive state of aquaristics and knowledge of coral biology at that time.

38. b) Dynamite is **not** used to collect ornamental fish. Unfortunately, cyanide use is widespread, mostly for live food fish for Asian markets. When dynamite is used it is used only to kill food fish. This tragic practice destroys reefs and fish stocks and must be stopped.

39. b) The porcupinefish is a member of the pufferfish family, Tetraodontidae. Like other members of this family, it has the ability to take in large amounts of water (or air, but air intake is not normal) and blow itself up into a large ball-like shape. In the case of the porcupinefish, each scale has a large spine that becomes erect when the fish is inflated. This creates a large, spiny ball that can discourage the most aggressive predator.

40. a) Bill Addison of C-Quest, Inc. began the commercial culture of Dottybacks in his hatchery in Puerto Rico in the early 1990's. He has been successful in rearing commercial numbers of many species of *Pseudochromis.*

41. Where was the Jaubert aquarium system developed?

　　a) Chicago

　　b) Java

　　c) Monaco

　　d) Hawaii

42. The whale shark, *Rhincodon typus*, is the largest know species of shark. Because of their great size, whale sharks cannot be kept in captivity.

　　a) True, the large size prevents capture and transport.

　　b) False, the Osaka Aquarium in Japan holds several specimens.

　　c) True, they can be captured but cannot be fed the vast amounts of plankton that they require in captivity.

　　d) False, small whale sharks are routinely kept with giant groupers.

43. This is a public aquarium world famous for its work with coral displays and coral reproduction.

　　a) Monterey Bay Aquarium, California

　　b) Osaka Ring of Fire Aquarium, Japan

　　c) Sydney Aquarium, Australia

　　d) Waikiki Aquarium, Honolulu, Hawaii

44. What is a Secchi disc?

　　a) an instrument scientists use to measure turbidity

　　b) the medial plate in a shark vertebrae

　　c) the small disk at the center of a starfish

　　d) the ring seen around a coral patch reef

41. c) Professor Jean Jaubert of the European Oceanographic Laboratory, has been developing coral mesocosms (contained environments that simulate the natural environment) at the Oceanographic Museum of Monaco. He patented a biological process that included a closed, water filled space, a "plenum", at the bottom of a relatively thick substrate in an aquarium system. This system functioned, among other things, to reduce nitrate (denitrify) in the system water to create a better "balance" and improve water quality. Dr. Jaubert's work, first introduced in the US by Tom Frakes, sparked extensive research by marine hobbyists into the advantages of deep substrates in marine systems.

42. b) There are very few whale sharks in captivity. They are trained to accept buckets of krill at certain places in the aquarium and can survive and grow in captivity. They may, however, outgrow the largest of tanks.

43. d) The Waikiki Aquarium, a center for research and education, is affiliated with the University of Hawaii. It was established as the Honolulu Aquarium in 1904 and is now under the direction of Dr. Bruce Carlson.

44. a) A Secchi disc is a black and white disc, about 30 cm in diameter, that is lowered into the water until it is no longer visible from the surface. The depth at which it disappears from view provides a measure of the turbidity of the water.

45. The world center for Tetraodontid dentistry is located in what city?

  a) Los Angeles

  b) Singapore

  c) Miami

  d) Louisville

46. What does Feng Shui have to do with marine aquaristics?

  a) In the Ming dynasty, Feng Shui was a famous fish keeper of the Emperors sea bass ponds.

  b) An aquarium can help the flow of good Chi.

  c) He developed the idea of the balanced aquarium in Japan.

  d) The Feng Shui filter captures organic molecules in a matrix of algal cells, which are then flushed from the system with air bubbles.

47. Where would you go to see the "Planet of the Jellies"?

  a) Monterey Bay Aquarium, California

  b) Osaka Ring of Fire Aquarium, Japan

  c) Sydney Aquarium, Australia

  d) Waikiki Aquarium, Honolulu, Hawaii

48. Where is the oldest marine only aquarium society in the US located?

  a) San Franscisco

  b) New York

  c) Miami

  d) London

45. d) You didn't know that there was a world center for Tetraodontid (puffer fish) dentistry, did you. It is located in the home of Kelly Jedlicki, a hobbyist with a passion for puffers. Kelly keeps about a dozen large puffers in various tanks that grow large and even spawn under her careful care. However, just as the beaks of some captive birds grow too long in captivity and have to be trimmed occasionally, the teeth of her puffers also need care. So Kelly and friends have developed a technique to anesthetize the puffers and grind down their teeth.

46. b) Feng Shui, pronounced "Fung Shway", is the ancient Chinese art of arranging one's surroundings to create the most favorable flow of Chi (energy). The plants, fish, rocks, and water sounds of an aquarium can contribute to this balance.

47. a) The Monterey Bay Aquarium pioneered the captive keeping and culture of jellyfish in the U.S. Their innovative jellyfish exhibit, "Planet of the Jellies" opened in 1992 and presented new culture, aquaristic techniques, and remarkable biological insights to the public.

48. c) The Florida Marine Aquarium Society meets in Miami and claims the title for the oldest, strictly marine aquarium society. It was founded in 1955 with Bob Straughan and Joe Turner, as a strictly marine aquarium society, not as an offshoot of a fresh water club. London? That's in England, dummy.

49. Which of these sharks can be kept in relatively small aquaria?

a) the nurse shark, *Ginglymostoma cirratum*

b) the bonnethead shark, *Sphyrna tiburo*

c) the whitespotted bamboo shark, *Chiloscyllium plagiosum*

d) the tiger shark, *Galeocerdo cuvier*

50. What is a plankton net?

a) the same as a food web, but in the plankton

b) a conical fine mesh net used to collect plankton

c) the annual production of plankton

d) the oral apparatus of a filter feeder

51. If you have a flamingo tongue, then what else should you have?

a) a large aquarium

b) a flamingo

c) a sea fan

d) a lot of turtle grass

52. How do aquariums control the growth of blacktip sharks in display tanks?

a) Small sharks are maintained until they outgrow the tanks and are then traded for smaller specimens.

b) No problem, sharks grow until they reach a limit set by the size of the tank and then stop growing.

c) The sharks are fed only enough to keep them healthy, but not enough to allow rapid and complete growth.

d) Hormones that prevent growth are added to the food.

49. c) Sharks are not the easiest of fish to keep in aquaria. Some species, such as the tiger shark, grow very large, require great roaming areas, and feed on large animals. Not a good choice for any type of aquarium. Of the small, relatively sedentary species, the whitespotted bamboo shark is one of the best species for small aquaria. Unlike the nurse shark, they do not grow large, maximum length about 38 inches, and they reproduce in captivity. Note that keeping any shark species, even those with a biology that is adaptable to captive situations, requires relatively large systems and strong commitment to the project.

50. b) Plankton nets are used by oceanographers and marine biologists to collect planktonic organisms for study, and by some fish and invertebrate breeders to collect food for larval culture.

51. c) The beautiful flamingo tongue cowrie, *Cyphoma gibbosum*, occurs all over the Caribbean and Bahamas. It has a creamy orange tinted shell which is usually covered with a mantle that has bright rectangular orange spots ringed in black. Unfortunately, it only feeds on gorgonians, mostly sea fans, so to keep it alive, an aquarist must have a never ending supply of sea fans.

52. c) Research at the Waikiki Aquarium found that by controlling food rations, the growth of black tip sharks could be controlled to limit growth in small tanks or by feeding up to 8 times the basic ration, more than double that growth rate.

53. MACNA is the acronym for

a) Marine Aquarium Council for National Action.

b) Maritime Action Conference for National Aquariums.

c) Marine Aquarium Conference of North America.

d) Meaningful Activities Colloquium for Nascent Aquarists.

54. When the Florida Marine Aquarium Society had their annual tank show, Eddie Steinman entered a novelty tank with baby *Gallus domesticus* in the center. How was this possible?

a) Another club member gave him the seedlings.

b) He collected them under a pier in the Keys.

c) An aquarium within an aquarium provided the right environment.

d) The *G. domesticus* were gradually adapted over weeks of time to be able to live in salt water.

55. Which is the longest Teleost (bony fish)?

a) whale shark

b) bluefin tuna

c) green moray eel

d) oarfish

56. A successful reproductive strategy is essential to the survival of a species. What fish employs parasitic males in its reproductive strategy?

a) deep sea ceratioid angler fish

b) Hawaiian cleaner wrasse, *Labroides phthirophagus*

c) the coral catfish, Plotosidae

d) twin spot gobies, *Signigobius biocellatus*

53. c) The first MACNA was held in Toronto, Canada on April 22, 1989. It was hosted by the Marine Aquarium Society of Toronto (MAST) and attended by marine aquarists from all over North America. The speakers were Helmut Debelius, Martin Moe, Albert Thiel, Peter Rubec, Tom Frakes, Forrest Young, and George Smit. The conference was very successful and the practice of holding an annual MACNA, hosted by various marine aquarium societies from cities all over North America, was born. MACNA XI was held in Louisville, KY on September 10 -12, 1999.

54. c) "Chicken of The Sea" was the name on his tank. *Gallus domesticus* are chickens! Eddie had baby chicks in a dry aquarium in the center of a saltwater aquarium. They pecked and scratched and the fish swam around them, an eye catching sight. (The chicks grew up and became pets of a club member.)

55. d) The oarfish, *Regalecus glesne,* can grow to over 50 feet (15 m) and lives in the deep water off the continental shelf. Although it is relatively thin, it is very long. A whale shark is not a bony fish, it is the largest cartilaginous fish, an elasmobranch.

56. a) Males in the deep sea ceratioid angler fish genera *Himantolophus* and *Melanocoetus*, are parasitic on the females, attaching to the females soon after metamorphosis. They then tie into the blood stream of the female and become little more than a male reproductive organ controlled by hormone levels in the blood of the female. And you feel tied down by your signigicant other?

57. What may be damaged if you break a calice?

a) your tail bone, at the end of your sitdown

b) the stony cup that surrounds a coral polyp

c) the metal halide light fixture over a reef tank

d) one of the arms of a fragile *Acropora* growth

58. Where are the horse latitudes?

a) This is another name for the equator.

b) between 30 and 45 degrees - where horses live best

c) wherever seahorses are found

d) between the equator and 30 degrees

59. Who/what was the famous "Feejee Mermaid" ?

a) the last member of a small, little known Indonesian native tribe that had webbed feet and lived intimately with the sea

b) a large manatee that was displayed at the first oceanarium, Marine Studios at Marineland, in St. Augustine, Florida in the 1940's

c) a hoax consisting of a the head and shoulders of a spider monkey attached to the body of a sea bass

d) a good friend of Jim Stime

60. Where is Reef Propagations (a salt water fish farm) located?

a) in a basement in a home in Chicago

b) near the shore in the Florida Keys

c) in England

d) in Hawaii

57. b) One must be careful not to hit coral fragments against each other or against hard objects, for the calice, the stony cup that protects each coral polyp, is easily damaged and when broken can lead to bacterial infection of the polyp. Also be sure to protect your coccyx, or sitting down may be difficult.

58. d) The latitudes between the equator and about 30 degrees are termed the horse latitudes. The reason for the name is obscure but these latitudes are often becalmed with very little wind for many weeks. In the days of sail, ships often carried horses to the new world and if they were without wind for too long, they would have to throw the horses overboard because their food supply was exhausted. Evidently this happened often enough for sailors to name these latitudes the "horse latitudes".

59. c) The "Feejee Mermaid" was displayed in a glass case by P.T. Barnum (who else) in his American Museum in the late 19th century. The same, or a similar display, was included more recently in Ripley's Believe it not Museum in St. Augustine, Florida.

60. a) Oh come on, a marine fish hatchery in a basement in Chicago, you've got to be kidding. Nope, we kid you not. Joe Lichtenbert has been producing many thousands of clownfish from the basement of his home for a number of years. It is very labor intensive, but Joe is very dedicated and has built quite an efficient hatchery in a small space.

61. Which is the mollusk with the poisonous beak?

    a) the amber pen shell, *Pinna carnea*

    b) the Atlantic pygmy octopus, *Octopus joubini*

    c) the fringe-back nudibranch, *Dondice occidentalis*

    d) the tulip snail, *Fasciolaria tulipa*

62. Which fish could be considered a hitch hiker?

    a) the remora, *Remora remora*

    b) the porcupinefish, *Diodon histrix*

    c) the queen triggerfish, *Balistes vetula*

    d) the French angelfish, *Pomacanthus paru*

63. Is it true that some large aquariums often use pigs for maintenance?

    a) False, this would be cruelty to animals.

    b) True, the pigs are pushed through the pipes to clean them - the pipes, that is.

    c) False, many aquariums have "lucky" pigs as pets, but they don't make them work.

    d) True, pigs are often used to clean up the snack areas after the visitors have left for the day.

64. Which of these fish is a "fisherman"?

    a) the yellowhead jawfish, *Opisthognathous aurifrons*

    b) the remora, *Echenesis naucrates*

    c) the spotfin flying fish, *Cypselurus furcatus*

    d) the stargazer, *Astroscopus y-graecum*t

61. b) Within the soft, bulbous head of the octopus is hidden a hard, horny beak with venom glands that inject prey organisms with a lethal toxin. The pygmy octopus carries enough toxin in its bite to make a human very sick and create a wound that is slow to heal.

62. a) The remora or sharksucker has a dorsal fin that is modified into a sucking disk. These fish swim with large predators and occasionally hitch a ride on their large companion by attaching, with the sucker apparatus on the top of their head, to the bottom, side, or even dorsal surface of the big guy. This puts them in the right place to feed on the dinner scraps the shark may scatter about when capturing prey. Remora make interesting aquarium inhabitants and are occasionally found in marine aquaria, usually in large tanks.

63. b) Actually the "pigs" in this case are fat little plastic projectiles that will just fit into the pipes and are pushed through the pipes under strong pressure. The "pigs" revolve as they speed through the pipes and remove the fouling organisms that grow on the inside of the intake pipes.

64. d) A fisherman baits his hook and waits for a bite. He or she offers a fish a tasty tidbit and then catches it when it "takes the bait". The stargazer burrows down in the sand with only the feathery fringes around the mouth showing through the bottom. When a small fish "takes the bait" and investigates these appetizing little fringes, the stargazer lets loose with 50 volts stunning the fish, and then the stargazer quickly snaps him up.

65. Which fish has three "sexes" (two types of males)?

a) the orchid dottyback, *Pseudochromis fridmani*

b) the bluehead wrasse, *Thalassoma bifasciatum*

c) the queen triggerfish, *Balistes vetula*

d) the French angelfish, *Pomacanthus paru*

66. Why does the cowry have such a shiny shell?

a) The varnish that the snail secretes keeps fouling organisms from growing on the shell.

b) A chemical released by the foot keeps the shell clean.

c) Cowries occur in large families and they clean each other constantly.

d) The mantle of the cowry is usually extended out over the shell and the secretions of this organ maintain a lustrous shell.

67. Who was the first to publicly display captive marine life in the U.S.?

a) P. T. Barnum

b) Bruce Carlson

c) Philip Henry Grosse

d) Dr. George Johnston

68. An unusual specimen of what species of angelfish sold for 50,000 rupees some time ago in a Zanzibar market? Typically, this fish sold for less than one rupee.

a) French angelfish, *Pomacanthus paru*

b) emperor angelfish, *Pomacanthus imperator*

c) half moon angelfish *Pomacanthus maculosus*

d) Koran angelfish, *Pomacanthus semicirculatus*

65. b) Many wrasses have two types of males, initial phase and terminal phase. In the case of the bluehead, the initial phase males are all yellow just like the females. Most initial phase (or primary) males develop directly into males after the juvenile stage and generally group spawn with many females. The terminal phase (or secondary) males are either females that have changed to males or initial phase males that have changed color. They have different and brighter colors than females and initial males. The terminal phase males tend to spawn one on one with individual females.

66. d) The mantle of mollusks takes many forms. In the cowries, it is a soft, tough protective tissue that glides completely over the shell. It is seldom retracted except when it is attacked by a predator. The mantle is often as brightly colored as the shell.

67. a) P.T. Barnum (1810-1891,"There's a sucker born every minute.") displayed aquariums and aquatic life in his American Museum in New York City as early as 1856. His collections helped establish the New York Aquarium which opened in 1896.

68. d) A juvenile Koran angelfish with mismarkings on the circular white bars turned up in a Zanzibar market. The misbarred fish seemed to have the words in Arabic characters *Laillaha, Illalahah* (There is no God but Allah) on one side and *Shani-Allah* (A warning sent from Allah) on the other. This specimen caused quite a stir and eventually sold for 50,000 rupees. Which is how this angelfish got the common name Koran angel.

69. FAMA is the acronym for

a) Family Aquarists in Marine Activities.

b) Future Aquarists of Marine America.

c) Freshwater And Marine Aquarium magazine.

d) Faustian Association of Marine Aquarists.

70. This world famous public aquarium was established in 1930 on the shores of a lake.

a) The John G. Shedd Aquarium

b) Theater of the Sea

c) Steinhart Aquarium

d) Steven Birch Aquarium-Museum

71. Coralline algae require calcium and strontium and will grow only on a calcareous substrate.

a) True, but only if ozone is also present.

b) False, because it can grow on almost all substrates.

c) True, because calcium is deposited on all substrates and this allows the coralline algae to adhere.

d) False, because it does not require strontium.

72. Where is one of the world's newest aquariums, with acrylic tunnels and a huge doughnut shaped tank, found?

a) Veracruz, Mexico

b) Toronto, Canada

c) Dallas, Texas

d) Miami, Florida

69. c) There are several periodicals for marine aquarists. FAMA (P. O. Box, 487, Sierra Madre, CA 91024) is one that has been in publication for many years. Others are Aquarium Fish Magazine (Fancy Publications, Inc., 3 Burroughs, Irvine, CA 92718), Marine Fish Monthly (Publishing Concepts Corp., Main Street, Luttrell, TN 37779), Tropical Fish Hobbyist (TFH Publications, Inc. One TFH Plaza, Neptune City, NJ 07753), and Sea Scope, (Aquarium Systems, Inc., 8141 Tyler Blvd, Mentor OH 44060). Faustian – Hmmm.. You don't know anyone who would sell their soul for a perfect reef tank, do you?

70. a) The John G. Shedd Aquarium is in Chicago, on the shores of Lake Michigan. Sea water for the marine displays was transported by railroad from the Gulf of Mexico (and also by barge along the Mississippi River) for many years.

71. b) Once conditions in a reef tank are suitable, coralline algae will grow on just about any substrate in the tank. A good growth of coralline algae is very desirable in a reef tank, and calcium and strontium are both required.

72. a) The Aquario Veracruz in Veracruz, Mexico has a huge, spectacular doughnut shaped tank with an acrylic tunnel entry and a lecture hall in the center surrounded by this great tank. It holds tarpon, nurse sharks, sea turtles, and other large sea life that circle around the visitors in the center of the tank.

73. If you have a triton, what do you also need?

    a) abundant algae

    b) a mermaid

    c) a starfish

    d) live rock

74. Which fish "swims in the sand"?

    a) the French angelfish, *Pomacanthus paru*

    b) the queen triggerfish, *Balistes vetula*

    c) the peacock flounder, *Bothus lunatus*

    d) the orangehead wrasse, *Halichoeres iridis*

75. Ecologists often lump fishes into guilds. What does this mean?

    a) Fish that construct burrows, like the masonic guilds of medieval builders, are grouped in guilds.

    b) This is a way of grouping fish according to their feeding habits.

    c) Fish are placed in guilds according to their reproductive modes.

    d) A guild is composed of fish that occupy the same ecological niche.

76. Who was the first to construct an all glass tank?

    a) Ross Socolof

    b) Dr. Herbert Axelrod

    c) Robert Straughan

    d) Dr. William T. Innes

73. c) The tritons, large marine gastropods in the genus *Cymatium*, prey largely on starfish. A trumpet triton, *C. variegata*, moving slowly along the sea floor may come across the trail of a giant starfish and then turn and begin a slow motion chase. It may take a day or more for the triton to catch the starfish, but in the end the triton captures and consumes the starfish just as a lion captures an antelope, but much more slowly.

74. d) The wrasses in the genus *Halichoeres* dive into the sand to escape predators and also spend the night buried in sandy sediments. They often enter the sand at one place and emerge at another, thus they exhibit the unusual behavior of "swimming in the sand".

75. b) The term guild is based on the concept of the medieval guilds of craftsman (masons, carpenters, glaziers, aquarists, etc.) and groups fish by the way they "make their living", that is, the way feed. There are algae browsers, coral browsers, plankton feeders, and predators of many types. OK, so there wasn't any medieval guild of aquarists. Sorry about that.

76. c) All of the above were pioneers in the tropical fish industry, but Bob Straughan has laid claim to building the first "all glass" tank held together with silicone rubber sealer. The history of his initial experimental work, with that of Ellis Skolfield, in building all glass tanks is described in the second edition of his book, *The Salt-Water Aquarium in the Home*, A.S. Barnes & Co., 1969.

77. What are sea lilies?

a) small plants that grow among the mangroves and have lily-like flowers

b) cowardly sharks (picked on by their peers)

c) deep sea echinoderms

d) a delicate Pacific jellyfish

78. What is the Breeders Registry?

a) This is an organization that keeps track of all offspring born to registered marine aquarists.

b) This organization provides pedigree papers to all owners of clownfish reared from registered pairs.

c) This organization keeps track of all liaisons that occur at various marine aquarist conferences.

d) This is a non profit organization that maintains and disseminates information on captive reproduction of marine organisms.

79. This coral has long sweeper tentacles and attacks nearby corals.

a) the elegance coral, *Catalaphyllia jardinei*

b) the mushroom anemone, *Discosoma* sp.

c) the sea fan gorgonian, *Gorgonia ventalina*

d) the branching corals, *Acropora* sp.

80. Which fish takes a blanket to bed every night?

a) the orchid dottyback, *Pseudochromis fridmani*

b) the blue parrotfish, *Scarus coeruleus*

c) the threadfin butterflyfish, *Chaetodon auriga*

d) the French angelfish, *Pomacanthus paru*

77. c) The sea lilies are crinoids, a type of deep sea, sessile echinoderm that can be very numerous in certain areas. Scientists study them by dredging them up or by observing and collecting them from deep sea submersible vehicles. Sea lilies are very numerous in the fossil record and all we can learn about species alive today helps us better understand the conditions that existed in ancient seas.

78. d) The Breeders Registry is open for membership to all marine aquarists, professional and amateur, that have an interest in propagation of marine organisms. US membership is $15.00, the address is P.O. Box 255373, Sacramento, CA 95865. Or check the web site

79. a) There is aggression among corals. Space is tight on a coral reef. Some corals war with sweeper tentacles studded with poison darts (nematocysts) to beat back their neighbors. Among the most aggressive corals are *Catalaphyllia, Euphyllia , Fungia, Goniopora* , and *Acropora. Acropora*, however, does not reach out to other corals with polyps or sweeper tentacles, rapid overgrowth is *Acropora's* weapon.

80. b) Many of the parrotfish, family Scaridae, secrete a mucus "blanket" about themselves when they nestle into the reef each night and this presumably protects the fish from predation. It takes the fish about 30 minutes to prepare the mucus blanket and about that long to remove it each morning. There are openings at the front and rear that allow water to flow through the blanket.

Index

The question page number is always listed in this index although the pertinent information may be found in the answer on the next page.

Index

Index

Index

Index

About The Authors

Martin Moe and Barbara Battjes met over a cup of coffee at Florida State University in September, 1959. Martin was a biology major and Barb a math and physics major. Barb made A's and Martin just sort of hung in there. By February of 1960 they were married, by March Barb was pregnant and Martin's grades improved greatly. After graduation and a year of teaching, Martin began his career as a marine biologist in 1961. Scott, Steve, and Andrea came along very quickly and the 60's and 70's had no dull moments.

Martin holds a masters degree from the University of South Florida and has worked as a fishery biologist, marine biologist, ichthyologist, and commercial marine fish breeder for over 35 years. His scientific and popular articles and books began in 1962 during his career as a marine biologist for the State of Florida. He entered the private sector in 1969 and developed the basic technology for breeding Florida pompano in 1970. Martin, with Barb's help, accomplished the first commercial culture of marine tropical fish (clownfish and neon gobies) in their garage in 1972, and over the years has reared over 30 species of marine tropical fish, including spawning, rearing, and even hybridizing French and grey Atlantic angelfish.Their latest rearing project was the propagation of the Red Sea orchid dottyback in a small fish room at home. This project became the book, *Breeding the Orchid Dottyback: An Aquarists's Journal.* Martin is also the author of a definitive book on tropical Atlantic lobsters, *Lobsters : Florida • Bahamas • the Caribbean*, as well as the popular and best selling marine aquarium books, *The Marine Aquarium Handbook : Beginner to Breeder* and *The Marine Aquarium Reference: Systems and Invertebrates.* They founded Aqualife Research Corporation in 1972 and Green Turtle Publications in 1982. Martin and Barbara recently moved to a beach front home in the Florida Keys where they will continue to write and publish books on marine life and aquarium topics, and work with experimental keeping and rearing of aquatic organisms.

Green Turtle Books

The Marine Aquarium Handbook :
Beginner to Breeder

A practical handbook on the theory and methods of
keeping and breeding marine tropical fish. Everything
you need to know to set up and maintain a successful
saltwater aquarium. Set up and maintenance, trouble
shooting, filtration, quarantine and disease, foods and
feeding, and even breeding are discussed in detail in
this best selling handbook. New edition revised and
expanded in 1992.

320 pages   ISBN 0-939960-07-9 $16.95

The Marine Aquarium Reference :
Systems and Invertebrates

A major reference for the modern aquarist. This book
contains text, tables, figures, and drawings that clearly
and simply explain the techniques and technology of
modern marine aquarium systems, including reef
systems. *The Reference* clearly explains and integrates
the new marine aquarium technology, trickle filters,
high intensity lighting, gas reactors, denitrifying filters,
protein foam skimmers, and many other advances with
the traditional, established techniques of keeping
marine aquariums. It also introduces the aquarist to the
latest classification of invertebrates and other living
organisms. This book is a companion volume to *The
Marine Aquarium Handbook* .

~~512 pages   ISBN 0-939960-05-2 $21.95~~ out of print

A new updated edition will be available in 2000
ISBN 0-939960-11-7

Green Turtle Books

Lobsters :
Florida • Bahamas • the Caribbean

This is a comprehensive reference to the natural
history, evolution, morphology, taxonomy, care and
culture, and the recreational and commercial fisheries
of the Caribbean spiny lobster, *Panulirus argus*. It
includes a detailed description of larval rearing
attempts on the the spiny lobster in the Florida Keys
and a synopsis of the world wide literature on rearing
and farming of spiny lobsters.

512 pages   ISBN 0-939960-06-0 $22.95

Breeding the Orchid Dottyback:
An Aquarist's Journal

In this book, Martin Moe brings you inside his home
fish room, his daily routine, and his every thought and
plan throughout a successful breeding project with the
Red Sea orchid dottyback. Spawning requirements and
behavior, larval rearing and feeding, food organism
culture, fish grow out and much more is described in
great detail in this book. It is more than a dry technical
manual, however, it is a daily journey through failure
and success leading to development of a workable
technique for rearing marine tropical fish.

288 pages   ISBN 0-939960-09-5 $19.95

Green Turtle Publications
P.O. Box 1800
Islamorada, FL 33036